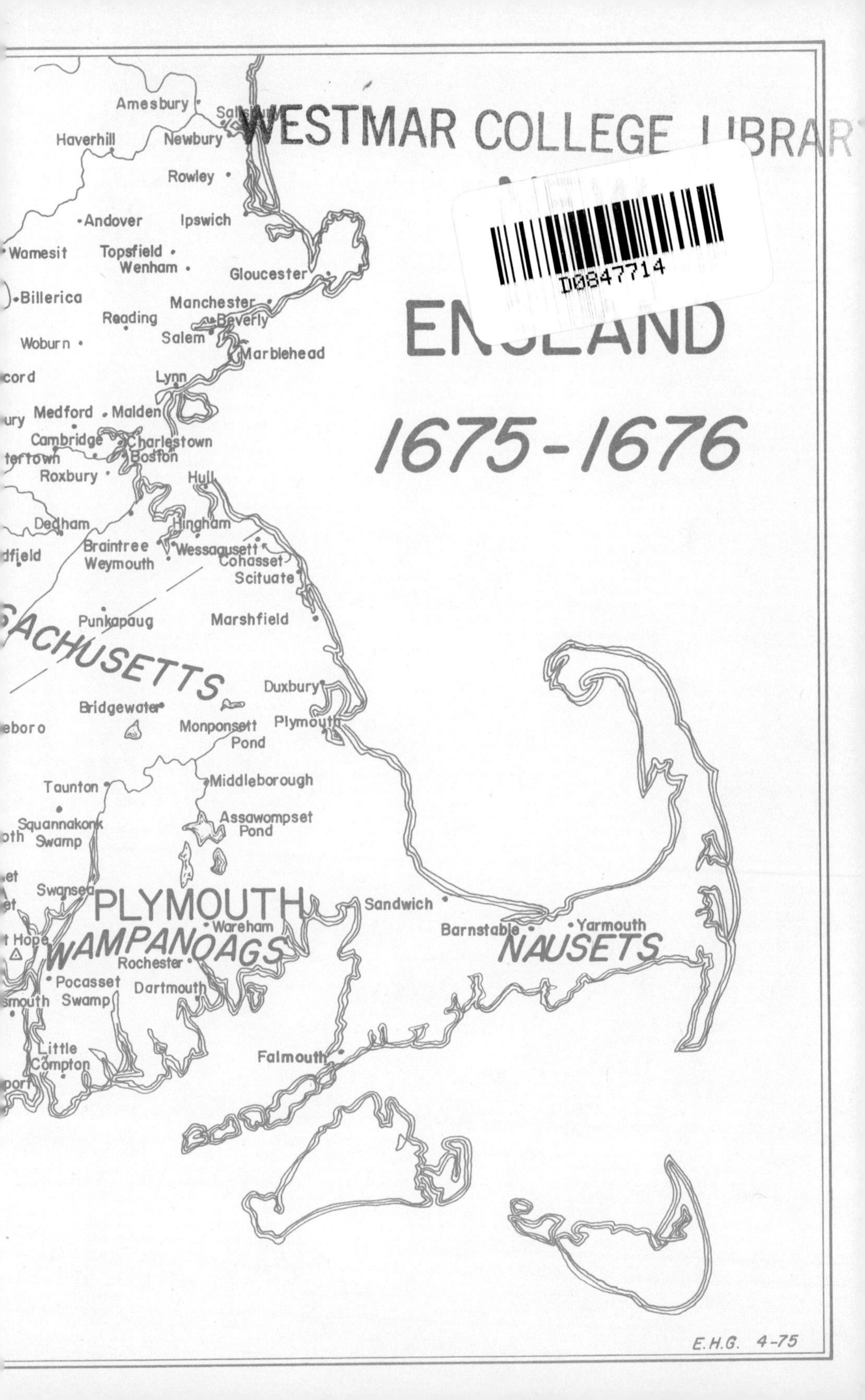
1675-1676
Amesbury
Haverhill
Newbury
Rowley
Andover
Ipswich
Wamesit
Topsfield
Wenham
Gloucester
Billerica
Manchester
Reading
Beverly
Salem
Woburn
Marblehead
Lynn
Medford
Malden
Cambridge
Charlestown
Boston
Roxbury
Hull
Dedham
Hingham
Braintree
Wessagusett
Weymouth
Cohasset
Scituate
Punkapaug
Marshfield
Duxbury
Bridgewater
Plymouth
Monponsett
Pond
Taunton
Middleborough
Squannakonk
Swamp
Assawompset
Pond
Swansea
PLYMOUTH
Sandwich
Wareham
Barnstable
Yarmouth
WAMPANOAGS
NAUSETS
Rochester
Pocasset
Swamp
Dartmouth
Little
Compton
Falmouth
E.H.G. 4-75

Diary of King Philip's War

BENJAMIN CHURCH.

DIARY OF KING PHILIP'S WAR

1675–76

by

Colonel Benjamin Church

with an
Introduction
by
Alan and Mary Simpson

A TERCENTENARY EDITION
1975

Published for the Little Compton
Historical Society

Chester, Connecticut 06412

DEDICATED

TO THE MEMORY OF

AWASHONKS

SQUAW SACHEM OF THE SOGKONATE INDIANS, COUSIN OF KING PHILIP, FRIEND OF BENJAMIN CHURCH

Library of Congress Catalog Card No. 74-27234

ISBN 0-87106-052-3

Manufactured in the United States of America

First Edition

Second Printing

Contents

Dedication *iv*

List of Illustrations *vii*

Foreword *xv*

Preface *xvii*

Introduction
by Alan and Mary Simpson 1

Entertaining Passages Relating to
Philip's War 67

Appendix I 179

Appendix II 181

Appendix III 187

Notes to Introduction 197

Notes to Text 203

Notes to Appendix I 215

Index 217

Illustrations

Paul Revere's Engraving of Benjamin Church. As reproduced in Samuel Drake's edition of 1827. Courtesy Boston Public Library, Boston, Mass. — Frontispiece

Wilbor House at Little Compton. — *xiv*

Fighting at Hadley, Massachusetts. Detail from John Seller's map of New England. — *xvi*

Indians in Dug-out Canoes. Details from William Blaeu's Map of New England, 1645. Courtesy of The John Carter Brown Library, Brown University. — *xxi*

Thomas Church's House at Little Compton. Built 1724, from a painting by George S. Burleigh, about 1880. Abby Maria Wilbour standing at the well; her daughter Evelyn C. Wilbour at the window; Charles Wilbour at gate. Courtesy of John G. Nelson, Jr. of Manchester, New Hampshire. — *xxiv*

John Leverett, Governor of Massachusetts. Courtesy of Essex Institute, Salem, Mass. — 3

Jabez Howland House, 1666, Plymouth, Mass. "The last house left in Plymouth whose walls have heard the voices of Mayflower Pilgrims." Jabez Howland was son of the Pilgrim, John Howland, and trusted — 4 lieutenant of Benjamin Church. Courtesy of the Pilgrim John Howland Society.

Champlain's Sketch of Wampanoag Wigwams at Plymouth, July 18, 1605; drawn by the explorer from the end of Beach Point. Courtesy of The John Carter Brown Library, Brown University. 5

Replica of Wampanoag Wigwam. Courtesy of Plimoth Plantation, Plymouth, Mass. 8

Ezra Stiles' Sketches of Niantic Wigwams in 1761. Courtesy of Yale University Library. The same manuscript volume of Stiles' Itineraries and Memoirs has other sketches of this wigwam, viz., an elevation view, indicating that its size was 17½′ x 12′, and a sketch of an iron pot of corn and beans suspended from the chimney by the double string and wooden hook which appears in this diagram. Stiles reports that sachems' wigwams used to be double-size, with two fireplaces. 9

Ninigret, Sachem of the Niantics. Only surviving 17th century painting of a New England sachem. Courtesy of Museum of Art, Rhode Island School of Design, Providence, R. I. 11

John Eliot, Preacher to the Indians. Courtesy of Henry E. Huntington Library and Art Gallery, San Marino, California. 13

Deed, with marks of Massasoit and his son Wamsutta, 29 March 1653. Conveys land near Mount Hope to Thomas Prince, Thomas Willitt, Myles Standish and Josiah Winslow, Courtesy of Mr. Henry Crapo, Register of Deeds, Taunton, Mass. 24

The First Purchase of Land from Awashonks by the Proprietors of Little Compton, 31 July 1673. Constant Southworth, William Pabodie, and Nathaniel Thomas represented the Proprietors. The deed is signed with the marks of Awashonks and her son Peter. Courtesy of Philip B. Wilbur, Town Clerk, Little Compton. 25

The John Alden House at Duxbury, Mass., where William Pabodie, a Proprietor of Little Compton, Married Betty Alden. Courtesy of Daniel Pearce, of the Alden Kindred of America, Inc. 37

Ruins of Benjamin Church's House at Bristol, circa 1880. Was located on north side of Constitution Street, near the corner of Thames Street. Courtesy of Massachusetts Historical Society, Boston, Mass. 40

Benjamin Church's Sword. Descended through his son Thomas, to his granddaughter Mrs. Mercy Richmond, who kept it by her bedside during the American Revolution. Given to the Massachusetts Historical Society by Mrs. Richmond's daughter, Mrs. Anne Atwood. 40

King Philip's Mark on a Deed of 1668. Courtesy of The John Carter Brown Library, Brown University. 42

Title Page of First Edition of Church's Diary, 1716. Courtesy of Boston Public Library, Boston, Mass. 45

Title Page of Second Edition, 1772. Courtesy of The John Carter Brown Library, Brown University. 48

Portrait of Ezra Stiles, Editor of Second Edition. By Samuel King 1771. Courtesy of the Yale University Art Gallery. 49

Model for Revere's Engraving of King Philip. Courtesy of Bradford F. Swan, *An Indian's an Indian,* The Roger Williams Press, 1959. 50

Revere's Engraving of King Philip. Courtesy of Bradford F. Swan, *An Indian's an Indian.* The Roger Williams Press, 1959. 51

Revere's Engraving of Benjamin Church (1772) and His Model, Mr. Charles Churchhill. Courtesy of The John Carter Brown Library, Brown University. 54

Engraving of King Philip from Drake's Edition of 1825. Courtesy of The John Carter Brown Library, Brown University. 56

Portrait of Samuel Drake, Editor of the "Third and "Fourth" Editions. Courtesy of Massachusetts Historical Society, Boston, Mass. 56

Portrait of Henry Martyn Dexter, Editor of the "Fifth" Edition. Courtesy of Massachusetts Historical Society, Boston, Mass. 58

A Nineteenth Century Engraving of King Philip. Courtesy of Philip Simonds, Little Compton. 60

Title Page of William Hubbard's Contemporary History of King Philip's War. Courtesy of The John Carter Brown Library, Brown University. 62

John Seller's Map of New England, 1675. Courtesy of The John Carter Brown Library, Brown University. 64

First Page of the First Edition, 1716. Courtesy of Boston Public Library, Boston, Mass. 68

Sakonnet. Drawn by Emily Garber, Vassar College. 71

Mount Hope and Pocasset. Drawn by Emily Garber, Vassar College. 76

Church's Sword; Leverett's Jerkin; Fitz John Winthrop's Armor; Andrus' Gun. Courtesy of Massachusetts Historical Society, Boston, Mass. 78

Sloop, about 1680. Drawn by W. A. Baker, Curator of the Francis Russell Hart Nautical Museum, Massachusetts Institute of Technology. 86

Statue of Massasoit, Plymouth. By Cyrus Dallin, 1921. Courtesy of L. D. Geller, Pilgrim Society, Plymouth, Mass. 87

Indians Cooking Fish. Drawing by John White. Courtesy of The John Carter Brown Library, Brown University. 93

Great Swamp Fight. Drawn by Emily Garber, Vassar College. 96

Palisaded Indian Village, Pomeiock, North Carolina. Drawing by John White, 1585. Courtesy of The John Carter Brown Library, Brown University. 97

Indians Fishing. Drawing by John White. Courtesy of The John Carter Brown Library, Brown University. 110

Treaty Rock, Little Compton. Photograph by Deneys Purcell. 111

Penelope Winslow, Wife of Governor Winslow. Courtesy of L. D. Geller, Pilgrim Society, Plymouth, Mass. 122

Josiah Winslow, Governor of Plymouth. Courtesy of L. D. Geller, Pilgrim Society, Plymouth, Mass. 123

Death of Philip. From an illustration in Daniel Strock, *Pictorial History of King Philip's War*, 1852. 152

Lock of Gun that Killed Philip. Courtesy of the Massachusetts Historical Society, Boston, Mass. 154

Philip's Seat at Mount Hope. Drawn by J. Neilson, engraved by A.B. Durand. Courtesy of Mrs. L. J. Giddings, Mount Hope. 155

The Cold Spring Monument at Mount Hope. Courtesy of Mrs. L. J. Giddings, Mount Hope. 157

Massasoit's Pipe. Otherwise known as King Philip's Pipe. A stone pipe with bear figure holding on to bowl. Found at Burrs Hill, Warren, R.I.—the "old Indian burial ground" of Church's Diary. Plaster copy given to Haffenreffer Museum of Anthropology, Bristol, R. I.; original at the Museum of the American Indian, Heye Foundation, N.Y.C. 164

Philip's "Samp" or Porridge Bowl. Courtesy of Katharine B. Edsell, Peabody Museum, Cambridge, Mass. 165

Niantic Mortar and Pestle. Courtesy of the Museum of the American Indian, N.Y.C. 165

Wampum. No extraordinary specimens of wampum from seventeenth century New England seem to have survived. These examples are reproduced by courtesy of the Museum of the American Indian, N.Y.C. 171

Indian weapons. Courtesy of *The Indians in Connecticut* by Chandler Whipple. The Berkshire Traveler Press. 1972. 171

Flintlocks of the Seventeenth Century. Courtesy of H. L. Petersen, *Arms and Armor of the Pilgrims 1620-1692.* Published by Plimoth Plantation and The Pilgrim Society. 175

Tombstones of Benjamin Church and His Wife Alice, Little Compton. Drawing by Sue W. Walker. 177

Lydia Tuspaquin. Mrs. Zerviah C. Mitchell, descendant of Massasoit, died 1895 at ninety at Betty's Neck, Middleboro, Mass. Courtesy of the Museum of the American Indian, N.Y.C. 178

Autographs of Benjamin and Joseph Church. 180

The William Pabodie House in Little Compton. Believed to have been built by William Pabodie, Proprietor of Little Compton and husband of Betty Alden. Courtesy of J. William Middendorf II. 196

Wilbor House at Little Compton.

Foreword

This book was published for the 300th Anniversary of King Philip's War by the Little Compton Historical Society with aid and encouragement from the Society of Colonial Wars in the State of Rhode Island and Providence Plantations.

We have undertaken this mission in honor of our ancestors and founders and in tribute to their friends and foes, the Indians of New England.

Our gratitude is given to Mary and Alan Simpson for introducing a new generation of readers to Ben Church's famous story. We know it has been a labor of love for them.

For the Little Compton Historical Society

Lawrence Lanpher, President 1972-1975
William S. Lynch, President 1969-1972
Philip B. Simonds, President 1963-1966
Carlton C. Brownell, Historian and Executive Director, President 1957-1960

For the Rhode Island Society of Colonial Wars

Stanley Henshaw, Jr., Governor
Bradford F. Swan, Historian
Lawrence Lanpher and Philip B. Simonds, Former Governors

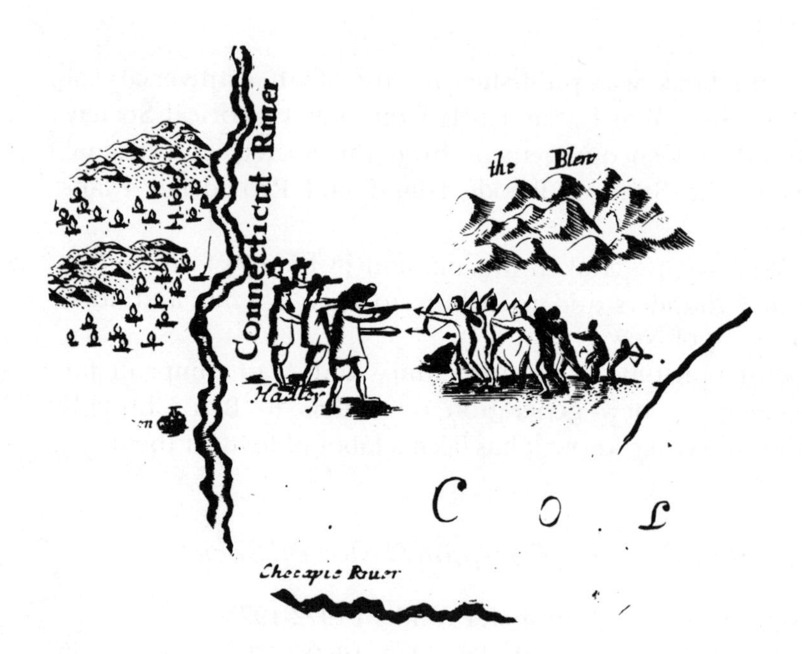

Fighting at Hadley, Mass.

Preface

Benjamin Church is Little Compton's village hero. We are reminded of him everywhere in the town and its neighborhood. He cleared a site on the south side of Windmill Hill when he was the first Englishman to settle in a neck of land full of Indians. He was bidden to a great dance of these Sakonnet Indians on the eve of the war—was it near Wilbour Woods or on the beaches?—where he found Awashonks, their queen, in a "foaming sweat" and Philip's men egging her on to war. His first skirmish with Philip's Indians was in Almy's pease field on Punkatees Neck. He left an invisible monument at Sakonnet Point, where he landed from a canoe to harangue a party of Sakonnet Indians who were fishing off the rocks; and a visible monument a few days later at Treaty Rock where he took their tribe out of the war. At the end of his life he built a house overlooking the Sakonnet River, just west of where his son Thomas' house still stands, and put together his memoirs there. He lies buried, in a file of family tombs, by the side of the church he helped to found.

Admiring his combination of vision, audacity, humanity and luck, and loving Little Compton almost as much as he did, we were delighted when we were asked by the Little Compton Historical Society to bring out a popular edition of his story to commemorate the tercentenary of the town. We were also under the spell of the long-gone race that had left stone bridges across our brooks, arrowheads in our soil, graves beneath our pavements and names on our streets. We were as eager to honor the Indian as the Englishman. We remembered that the bicentenary of King Philip's War, in 1875, had led to the erection of the Cold Spring Monument on Mount Hope to mark the place where Philip was killed, and we thought it would be appropriate if this tercentenary edition of 1975 should be dedicated to Awashonks, squaw-sachem of the Sakonnet Indians, who was both Philip's cousin and Church's friend.

Without the help and indulgence of many friends it would never have been possible to finish this work in the intervals of college life. Would that we could mention them all!

We are deeply indebted to the officers of the Little Compton Historical Society and of the Rhode Island Society of Colonial Wars—to William S. Lynch, who invited us to undertake this edition, to Lawrence Lanpher, whose constant help has seen it to the end, to Philip B. Simonds, whose idea it was in the first place, to Bradford F. Swan for invaluable counsel, and to Carlton C. Brownell for his unique mastery of local history. Carl and Carol Haffenreffer have been a never-failing source of inspiration and encouragement from beginning to end. Appeals to David Patten, J. William Middendorf II, Philip B. Wilbur, Virginia Lynch, John Nelson, Nathaniel B. Atwater, John C. Burchard and other Little Compton residents or visitors have always been generously met.

At Vassar College we remember affectionately Constance Dimmock Ellis, whose villa at Churriana in Spain was the scene of our first scribbles in 1971, Jean and Ralph Connor, who braced us for the final struggles at their Bequia home in the West Indies in 1974, Elizabeth Runkle Purcell, Chairman of the Board, and her fellow trustees who granted us a semester's leave of absence in 1974, George D. Langdon, Jr., Jerry W. Frost and Jonathan Clark, our colleagues in the Department of History who are experts in this field, and those angels in the President's office, Velma Gooding, Ethel Grauer and Angie Smith who cheered us on with typewriters, tallyhos and cups of tea.

We owe a special debt to Carlisle Humelsine, President

of Colonial Williamsburg, to our colleagues on the board there and to its highly imaginative staff, all of whom share our interest in the endeavor to recreate today the thoughts and feelings of the founders of America.

A goodly company of libraries, museums and historical societies have offered their hospitality: the Thompson Memorial Library at Vassar College; the Haffenreffer Museum of Anthropology at Bristol, R.I.; the John Carter Brown Library, the Rockefeller Library, the Public Library and the Rhode Island Historical Society in Providence; the Massachusetts Historical Society and the Public Library in Boston; the Houghton Library at Harvard and the Peabody Museum; the Yale University Library; the Library of the College of William and Mary at Williamsburg; the Museum of the American Indian and the New York Historical Society in New York City; the Pilgrim Society and Plimoth Plantation in Plymouth, the American Antiquarian Society in Worcester, Mass.; the Essex Institute at Salem, Mass.; the Bronson Museum at Attleboro, Mass.; the Duxbury Rural and Historical Society, the Tiverton (R.I.) Historical Society, the Bristol (R.I.) Historical Society, the Warren (R.I.) Historical Society, the Pettaquamscutt (R.I.) Historical Society and many other historical societies throughout the New England theater of King Philip's War.

Acknowledgements are due to the historians, ethnohistorians, anthropologists and archaeologists who are providing new insights into the collision of cultures which lies behind the war. Among them Douglas E. Leach, Alden T. Vaughan, Wilcomb Washburn, Francis Jennings, Neal Salisbury, W. S. Simmons, Catherine Marten and our friends at the Institute of Early American History and Culture, Thad Tate and Norman S. Fiering, have been especially stimulating.

In the preparation of illustrations we have had the expert help of Thomas R. Adams of the John Carter Brown Library, William A. Baker of the Francis Russell Hart Nautical Museum in Cambridge, Mass., Miss Jeanette Black of the John Carter Brown Library Henry Crapo, Registrar of Taunton, Jane Dwyer of the Haffenreffer Museum Katherine B. Edsell of the Peabody Museum, William S. Fowler, of the Massachusetts Archaeological Society, Malcolm Freiberg of the Massachusetts Historical Society, L. D. Geller of the Pilgrim Society, Carmelo Guadagno of the Heye Museum, Mrs. Lewis J. Giddings of the Haffenreffer Museum, J. William Middendorf II, Secretary of the Navy, John G. Nelson, Jr. of Manchester, New Hampshire, Peggy Nelson of the Essex Institute, Salem, Mass., Daniel Pearce of Duxbury, Mass., William Ridgeway of Fisher's Island and Mystic Seaport, Bradford F. Swan of Providence, Deneys Purcell of Cambridge, Mass., Ella and Eric Thomas of Plimoth Plantation, Sue W. Walker and Philip B. Wilbur of Little Compton, Ellen Wilson of the Haffenreffer Museum, Betts Burroughs Woodhouse and Roger Vaughan of Little Compton, and Alexander O. Vietor of the Yale University Library.

The credit for raising our sights from six illustrations to sixty goes to our good friend Chandler Hill, of the Pequot Press. But how sorry we are after all these adventures with illustrations that a book about swamp warfare will appear without a picture of a swamp! We have no problem in visualizing a swamp. Our land is full of them. But they are not photogenic. All we can offer is the explanation of a Boston reporter in 1676 whose London readers knew all about Yorkshire moors and Irish bogs but who were not used to seeing them studded with oaks, maples, pines and hollies or choked with brush and briars.

"A swamp signifies a Moorish Place overgrown with Woods and Bushes, but soft like a Quagmire or Irish Bogge, over which Horse cannot at all, nor English Foot (without great difficulty), passe." (Nathaniel Saltonstall *A New and Further Narrative of the State of New England,* London 1676.)

There is no skirmish, ambush or assault in this story which does not occur in or near a swamp. Swamps were the Indians' sanctuary until Englishmen like Church invaded them.

Alan and Mary Simpson
Yellow Gate Farm, Little Compton
President's House, Vassar College
April 1975

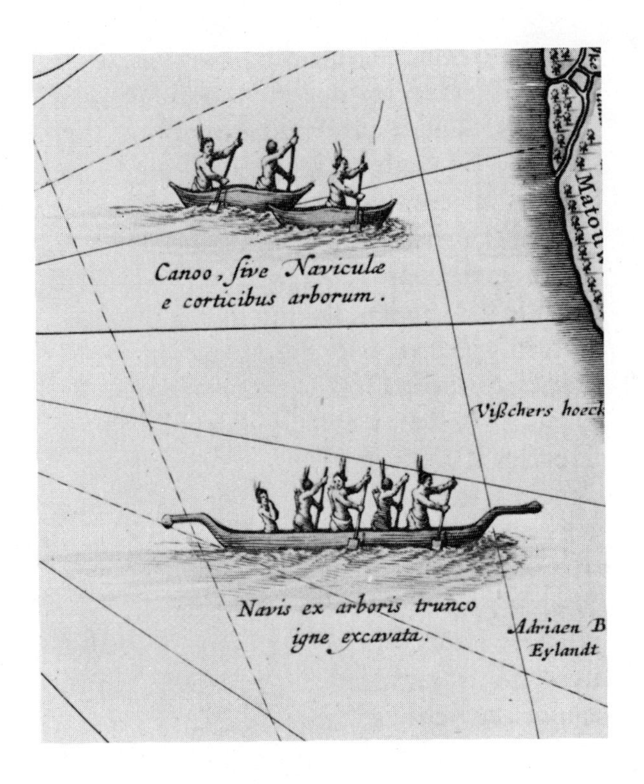

Indians in Dug-out Canoes.

Diary of King Philip's War

Thomas Church's House at Little Compton.

Introduction

King Philip's War of 1675-76, which is the subject of Benjamin Church's memoirs, was the final tragedy in the relations between the Indians of New England, whose ancestors had roamed the continent for millenia, and the English invaders who had first landed at Plymouth in 1620. As in Virginia, where a similar history had unfolded in much the same period, an aboriginal culture which was vigorous and flourishing in 1600 was almost totally destroyed by 1700. Benjamin Church's diary of King Philip's War—for that is what his memoirs are—opens with no more introduction than the explanation that he was clearing a homestead in Little Compton when the storm clouds broke. Behind his homely stories of the Pease Field fight, the Great Swamp fight, the parleys with Queen Awashonks, and the execution or capture of King Philip and all his captains, lies a collision of cultures which set the pattern for almost all future relations between white men and red men in English America.

The purpose of this Introduction is to explain how this warfare of extermination, which nobody had planned, took place; how a settler in Little Compton became an expert in Indian warfare and the conqueror of Philip; how his story has come down to us; and what may be thought of its historical value. Its human interest will speak for itself.

Collision of Cultures

At the outbreak of war in June 1675 there were one hundred and ten little towns or plantations in New England, dotted along the coasts and spreading up the rivers among the inland forests and swamps—sixty-four in Plymouth and Massachusetts, twenty-three in Connecticut, six in Rhode Island, four in New Hampshire, thirteen in Maine. Massachusetts, with a population conservatively estimated at 17,000, had its urban capital at Boston with villages ringed around until the outermost ring was reached with Dunstable, Groton, Lancaster, Marlborough, Menden and Wrentham. Beyond these frontier towns the trails ran through the Nipmuck country where the only white villages were two isolated outposts, Quinsigamond (Worcester) and Quabaug (Brookfield). Plymouth Colony had a population of about 5,000, with Dartmouth, Swansea and Rehoboth reckoned as frontier towns. The 10,000 settlers in Connecticut were mostly scattered along the Long Island Sound or up the Connecticut River. Rhode Islanders may have amounted to 3,000 or 4,000. These figures would put the total white population of New England in 1675 no higher than 36,000 to 45,000, which is the approved guess today, as compared with estimates of older historians which ran as high as 80,000. Plymouth, the earliest settlement, was at this date fifty-four years old, Boston forty-four, Providence thirty-eight.

Benjamin Church, pioneering from Duxbury, had just built the first homestead in Little Compton. The leadership of the earliest generation of founding fathers had passed away, except for a few giants in their seventies like Roger Williams and John Eliot, Josiah Winslow, the son of Edward Winslow, was the Governor of Plymouth Colony. John Leverett was the Governor of

John Leverett, Governor of Massachusetts.

Massachusetts. John Winthrop, son of the first Governor of Massachusetts, was Governor of Connecticut. A learned ministry, recruited from England and from Harvard College, was serving nearly one hundred churches. Over eighty of these were regular Congregational churches; six or seven were missionary Indian churches; six in Rhode Island were Baptist churches and one was Quaker. Land was being bought, cleared, developed, settled and sold on the expanding frontiers.

This was a resourceful, self-confident community of farmers, lumbermen, traders, fishermen, sailors, craftsmen, schoolmasters, ministers—with a raffish fringe of misfits, drunks and adventurers. The best of them had a civic spirit that was English, a Puritan sense of vocation, and an uncommon capacity for getting things done. They were the heirs and progenitors of whatever was progressive in the Western civilization of their day.

These white men had intruded themselves on lands that were now sustaining about 20,000 Indians—roughly half the number of the white settlers in 1675, if the modern guesses are reliable. They all belonged to the same language group—the Algonquians—so they could understand each other easily enough, but they were distributed in various nations, each with its own name and territory, and these nations were in turn made up of loosely associated tribes. Tribes were settled in one or more villages or towns and governed by their sachems, who might meet in a council of sachems for confederate purposes or even pay tribute

Jabez Howland House, Plymouth, 1666.

to a chief sachem. The sachem was an hereditary chief, drawn from a leading family, whose office could descend to a woman in the absence of a male heir. The religious leaders, or powwows, came from the same group of families. Rivalries among tribes, and among confederations of tribes, produced patterns of power politics similar to those which existed among the autonomous states of the Old World, except that the scale was so much smaller.

The Wampanoags, though not the largest or most powerful of the major groups in southern New England, were the first to take up arms. Under Massasoit, who had welcomed the Pilgrim Fathers and remained at peace with their colony for forty years, the territory of the Wampanoags and their satellites extended from the middle of the Narragansett Bay to Plymouth, Cape Cod and Martha's Vineyard. Surrounding them were the Narragansett tribes on the west, the Nipmucks to the northwest, the Massachusetts to the north, and the Nausets on Cape Cod. The ancestral seats of the chief sach-

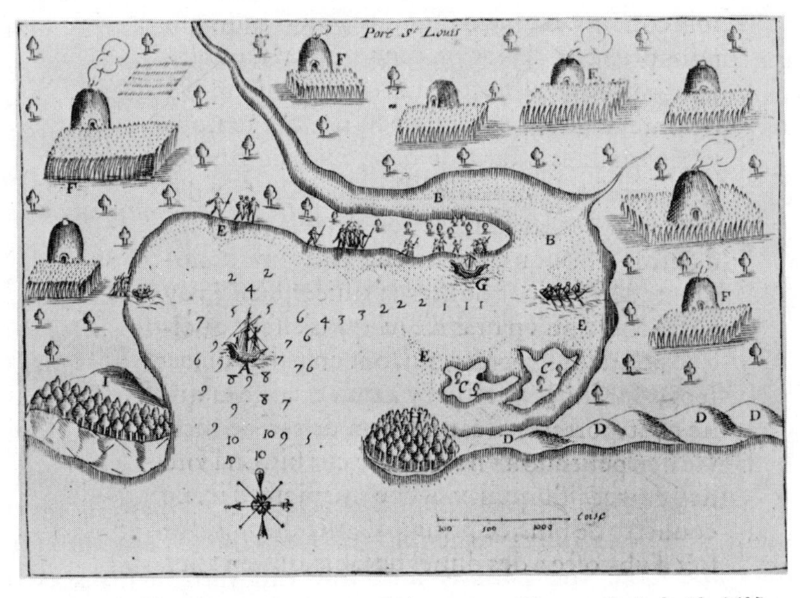

Champlain's Sketch of Wampanoag Wigwams at Plymouth, July 18, 1605.

em of the Wampanoags were on Mount Hope Neck—at Sowams, where Warren now stands, another on the bank of the Kikemuit River, and a third on Mount Hope itself. The Wampanoags, like all the Indians in southern New England, rotated their quarters with the seasons, as planting, hunting, fishing, and winter-shelter dictated. Massasoit's territorial authority—his overlordship—ebbed and flowed with the tides of politics, battle and disease, but the effective inner circle was bounded by an arc which swept through Rhode Island, Providence, Rehoboth, Taunton, Bridgewater and Middleboro down to Buzzard's Bay. Under his two sons, the westward expansion of the colonists from Plymouth turned Wampanoags from friends into enemies. Alexander, or Wamsutta, the elder son, died mysteriously, after a show of protest. Philip, or Metacomet, the younger son, became the spearhead of the general insurrection.

It may be that Philip, at the height of his power, commanded no more than 300 fighting men in his own tribe, which would have brought its numbers to about 1,200, counting women and children. This was the best guess of William Hubbard, the Boston clergyman who wrote a contemporary history of the war. But what was Philip's "tribe"? How many underlords did it include? Annawon had his headquarters in the Squannaconk Swamp between Rehoboth and Taunton. Tispaquin was "the black sachem" of the Assawompsett Pond. Tyasks and Totoson each had their settlements to the south. All four were famous captains who were to die on Philip's side. Was Hubbard including all of them? And who was Church including when he stated, after the war, that about 1,300 of King Philip's men, women and children had been either killed or captured?

Precision is impossible. But clearly no one would include among King Philip's people the Wampanoags on Cape Cod, the islands and the Vineyard, who stayed out of the war. Hubbard also makes it clear that he was not including two tribes across the river from Mount Hope, each closely linked with Philip by kinship and alliance and each presided over by a woman. The nearest of the two, in what is now Tiverton, were the Pocassets, commanded by their squaw-sachem Weetamoo. Her first husband was King Philip's older brother Alexander, whom she no doubt believed had been poisoned by the English. Her second husband, Peter Nunnuit, as the English called him, threw in his lot with the colonists when the war broke out, but she stuck to Philip and married, as her third husband, Quinnapin, the Narragansett sachem. An unforgettable sketch of her has been left by the wife of a Congregational minister, Mrs. Rowlandson, who spent nearly three months as a prisoner in the hands of the Indians and had to endure the cuffs and curses of Weetamoo, her "mistress," until she was eventually ransomed: "a severe and proud dame she was, bestowing every day in dressing herself neat as much time as any of the gentry of the land. . . . Her arms from her elbows to her hands were covered with bracelets; there were handfuls of necklaces about her neck, and several sorts of jewels in her ears. She had fine red stockings, and white shoes, her hair powdered and face painted red."[1]

She was to perish at the end of the war in the slaughter which engulfed almost all of Philip's relatives.

To the south of the Pocassets, on the neck of land where Benjamin Church was settling, the squaw-sachem Awashonks, a cousin of Philip's, presided over the Sakonnet Indians. Their winter headquarters was an upland mound in Tompe Swamp, north of the present Swamp Road, Little Compton, where her memory is preserved in what is now Wilbour Woods. She had made a submission to Plymouth Colony after a war-scare in 1671 and had sold lands to the Sakonnet Proprietors, among them Benjamin Church, in 1673. Many of the most vivid sketches in Church's memoirs are of her and her people.

To the northwest of Mount Hope, in the 15,000 square miles of wilderness which stretched between the rings of settlements around Boston and the thin ribbon of villages on the Connecticut River, was another major group of Indians, the Nipmucks of central Massachusetts. No one knows whether they had originally been a single nation or a confederacy, but they were clearly a prey to powerful neighbors when the whites arrived. The Narragansetts, the Massachusetts, the Pennacooks,

Replica of Wampanoag Wigwam, Plimoth Plantation.

the Pequots and the Mohawks had all exacted tribute from one village or another. In 1664, their titular head had put himself under the protection of the Wampanoags. By the eve of King Philip's War there may have been as many as 3,000 members of the tribe, scattered in larger or smaller bands over hundreds of square miles, each with its own sachem, who might confer with others in times of peril and come under the influence of the strongest personalities. In the coming war, after the English

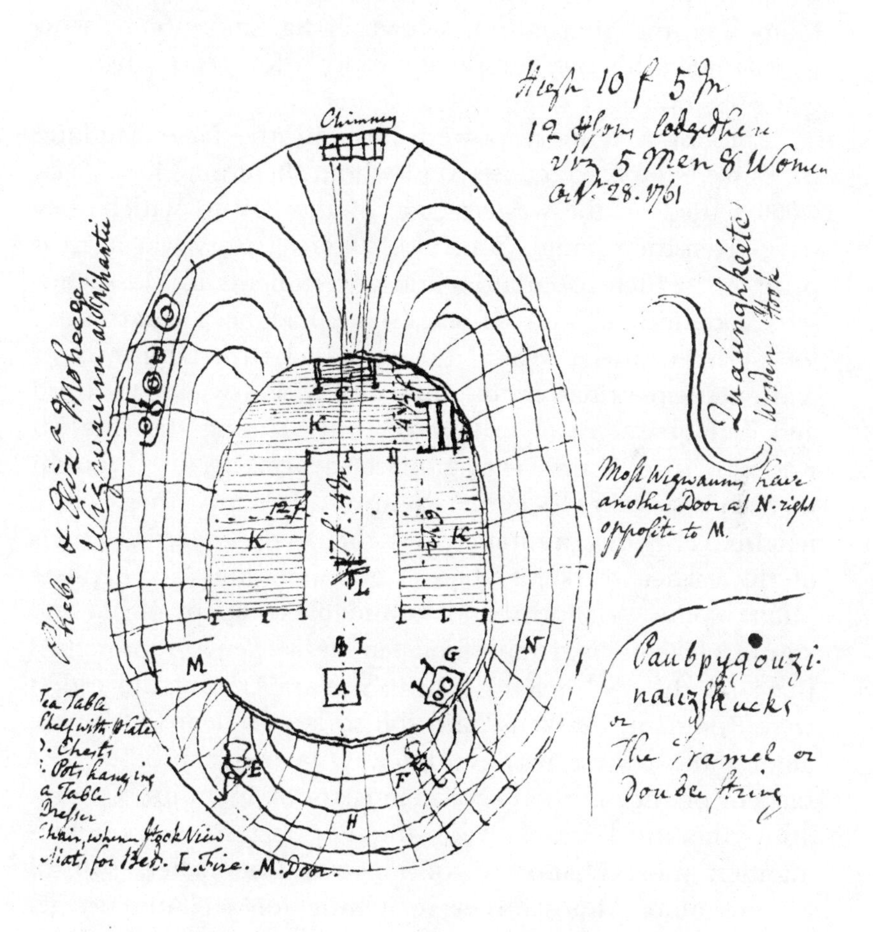

Ezra Stiles' Sketches of Niantic Wigwams in 1761.

had missed their chance of bottling up Philip in his own territory, the area around Mount Wachusett was to be the wilderness fastness from which Nipmucks, Wampanoags and Narragansetts launched their raids against both the frontier towns of Boston and the towns on the Connecticut River. Famous names among the sachems of the Nipmucks were Muttaump of Quabaug (Brookfield), a leader of the pro-war party; Matoonas, who led the attack on Mendon; Monoco, otherwise known as One-Eyed John, who led the attack on Groton and lived to betray and kill Matoonas; and Shoshanim, known as Sagamore Sam, who was to make his own desperate appeals for peace once the game was up.

Largest and most powerful of all the New England tribes were the Narragansetts, of whom there may have been 4,000 settled on the western side of the bay to which they have given their name. Control of their territory was a great prize over which speculators and governments in Massachusetts, Connecticut and Rhode Island had been quarrelling for at least fifteen years, during which time outposts of white settlement had been established at Warwick, Wickford and Pettaquamscut. The lack of unity among the English was not lost on the Narragansett sachems as they fought their endless struggles either for survival against their white neighbors or for dominance over their red. The great chiefs of the earlier years had been Canonicus and his nephew Miantonomo. A colorful and formidable company of old and young sachems, and male and female sachems, represented them on the eve of King Philip's War. Among the oldest were Pumham, Pessacus, and the squaw-sachem Quaiapen; among the wiliest was Ninigret, Quaiapen's brother, the sachem of the southern Narragansetts or Niantics; Quinnapin, the third husband of the Pocasset Weetamoo was another; most glamorous of all was Canonchet, son of Miantonomo. Almost all were itching for a chance to get even with the English, but for Ninigret loyalty to the English was self-preservation.

Among the remaining groups who made up the 20,000 Indians in southern New England, two others—enemies of the Narragansetts—had found it to their interest to follow an Anglophile policy. These were the once-powerful Pequots and their Connecticut neighbors, the Mohegans, who had built their own ascendancy on the ruins of Pequot power under their sâchem, Uncas. Others like the Massachusetts around Boston had been too weakened by disease to resist the colonists—their rulers became protected sachems in "praying-towns" like Natick.

Ninigret, Sachem of the Niantics.

As the English surveyed these native inhabitants, what did they think of them? Many things, no doubt, and different things for different people, but, in general, the Indian was a heathen savage, to be liked for his kindness, feared for his treachery, admired for his skills, respected for his moments of dignity, and pitied for all his inferiority to civilized Christians—a poor savage in times of peace, a diabolical savage in times of war. After all, he lived in dark, smoky, smelly wigwams, went naked or in skins before the English sold him coats and blankets; and ate his food with his fingers. To many of his best friends among the English he often seemed little better than a beast. The grasping colonist exploited him, selling dear the guns, hatchets, knives, pots, trinkets and liquor, which the Indian wanted, while buying cheap his furs and his lands. "For a copper kettle and a few toys, such as beads and hatchets," John Smith had said in his *Advertisements,* "they will sell you a whole country." The unceremonious pioneer had sometimes been struck by the Indian's "stateliness," his "graveness," his habit of bowing when he excused himself from an unacceptable request. This formal courtesy could be charming, but it wore off. The same Indian could become a nuisance and a menace. Memories of black looks, thefts, and murderous forays cast a shadow over his friendliest appearances, and terrifying tales were told of his habits in war. The ordinary English householder, after the sense of dependence and the novelty had gone, usually wanted as little to do with him as possible.

A basic emotion, conscious or unconscious in the English mind, was the fear of massacre. Once established in their plantations, they never doubted their power to overwhelm the Indian, if it came to a test of strength. In Virginia, John Smith had even boasted that with forty men he could bring them "all in subjection." But it was also in Virginia that Englishmen had suffered terrible losses at the hands of Indians in 1622 and again in 1644, and no New

Englander ever forgot it. It took more time for these seventeenth-century ancestors of modern Western man to develop their technological muscles than we can easily remember today.

If a sense of superiority could produce condescension and contempt, it could also stimulate a sense of obligation. The duty to protect, educate, improve and convert the Indian was given lip service by the Puritan establishment and yeoman service by a few great spirits. To a "seeker" like Roger Williams, most of the so-called Christians were as lost in spiritual darkness as the heathen Indians. He was not a missionary to the Indian, but he befriended him, published a key to his language, upheld his interests, and won his trust. John Eliot began the missionary enterprise in the

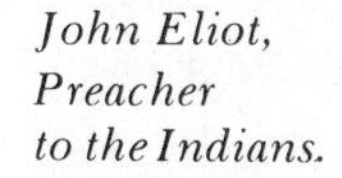
John Eliot, Preacher to the Indians.

forties. He set up the first "praying-village" in 1651. By the outbreak of war there were fourteen in Massachusetts. At the most famous of these, Natick, Sassamon had been educated and had taught as a schoolmaster. This was the Indian who betrayed Philip's plans to the Plymouth government and whose execution, at Philip's command, started the war.

An enthusiastic visitor from Europe wrote of the Christian Indians, "These go clothed like the English, live in framed houses, have flocks of hogs and cattle about them, which, when they are fat, they bring to the English markets."[2] He added, that some of their sons went to Harvard, but few of them stayed the course. There was room enough in the house that was built in Cambridge for Indian students to accomodate the press that printed the Indian Bible.

What Eliot was doing in Massachusetts, Bourne and Leverich were doing in Plymouth and the Mayhews on Martha's Vineyard and Nantucket. Daniel Gookin gave a breakdown of the distribution of praying Indians in a pamphlet which was published a few months before the war began. He showed 1,150 in Massachusetts, 462 in Plymouth and 1,500 on the islands. Bourne had reported a year earlier that 142 of the praying Indians in Plymouth could read their own language, seventy-two could write it, and nine could read English. Estimates of the total number of praying Indians ran as high as 4,000 — most of them concentrated on the islands and around the seaboard towns, while the powerful tribes resisted the movement and the remoter tribes were untouched.

The missionary enterprise had its ambiguities, then as always, where cultures of unequal strength are involved. Its appeal to the power-seeker and to the acquisitive among the English, as well as to the pure of heart, was not lost on the "heathen savage."

Over and above the attitudes of individual Englishmen to Indians, there was the Indian policy of the colonial governments. This had been based, since the Pequot War of 1637, on the assumption that the red man must conform to the white man's law. The tribe within reach of English authority was required to accept the status of a protected people, and its chiefs were called in to renew their submission whenever there was any suspicion of trouble. Individual Indians were held responsible for their misdeeds in English courts, and efforts were made to make the tribe accountable for the acts of its members.

The pressure of English authority can no doubt be exaggerated. It was not intended to be provocative. It was handicapped by poor communications and by all the other factors which deprive elective officials of consistency of purpose. But it was axiomatic that the white man should not show weakness in the face of the red man, and force was threatened whenever it was necessary to secure submission.

Familiar as we are with the tyranny of white Americans over blacks, we can recognize that Puritan governments were protected by their standards from falling into some of the worst forms of racism. An Indian could be admitted to an Englishman's church. He could get a conviction against an Englishman in an English court, even though Indians complained that their testimony was not taken as seriously as that of white men. Paternalistic legislation was passed for his benefit in matters of land as well as morals. The Puritan's sense of sin and the Englishman's sense of justice offered securities against several sorts of arbitrariness. At the same time, we must not forget that the self-righteousness of the Puritan, which was nursed on a doctrine of predestination and on a study of the Old Testament, opened up other temptations. Sufficiently goaded, the clergy could discover a duty to exterminate the ungodly heathens if they interfered with the enjoyment of the Promised Land by God's Chosen People. And it was only the rarest of Puritans who perceived that these people who did not wear clothes had a sense of honor at least as tender as his own.

What the Indian thought of the Englishman has to be reconstructed from second-hand sources. Scribblers on the English side, the Reverend William Hubbard, Increase Mather, Mary Rowlandson and others, were keeping a record for posterity while the war was being fought. Hubbard's narrative, the best of all of them, came off a Boston press in 1677 and a London press a few months later. But there were no scribblers on the Indian side. Their quizzing of missionaries, their complaints in parley, the sayings of their powwows, their taunts in battle, their postures in victory and defeat, have sometimes come down to us, but always with the brevity of an oracle or an anecdote. "That is my father's wigwam," says a friendly Indian fighting at Church's side, "am I to kill my father?"[3]

What would a historian give to have a record of Annawon's conversation with Church in the night which ended the war! In the three centuries which have passed since the Indian's fate in New England was sealed, it has often been remarked that his history has been written by his enemies.

But sentiment can be as deceiving as prejudice. What are we to make of the "friendly" Indians? Their numbers, credentials and loyalty are too impressive to allow us to think of them as ignoble collaborationists. What the "friendly" Indian reflected was such factors as the absence of any real unity among the Indians, the play of power politics which forced the weaker tribe, such as the Mohegans or the Pequots, to seek English protection, the susceptibility of some Indians to the civilizing mission of the English and of others to the appeal of the successful captain. And always, of course, there was the operation of a code of honor which sanctioned conduct which another culture might find discreditable.

It was a friendly Indian, Alderman, who shot down Philip and carried off his severed hand "to get him many a penny."[4] It was an Indian who led Church to Annawon's camp while asking to be excused from killing his old friend.

It was an Indian who showed the English how to reach and storm the Narragansett fort in the Great Swamp. Were such as these saving their skins? Or thinking of some larger ends? Or simply discharging a warrior's code of service? Performing a duty in return for a life that had been spared? Accepting a new captain with a cheerful conscience? The ties which Church could forge between himself and Indian fighting men were certainly of this last kind.

Of course, we cannot penetrate their ultimate feelings. But we must recognize that many Indians could organize their loyalties around personal, professional or tribal ends in ways which often seemed to ignore the claims of race as such. The record of Indian grievances which has come down to us in English writings shows no power to generalize. If there was a general idea, such as an idea of Indian nationalism, to fuse all the particular resentments into a white heat of rational commitment, it does not come through to us. There is no Indian Jefferson to tell us what truths he held to be self-evident. Yet, having said this, we must also acknowledge that during the seventeen months of fiery confrontation which Philip's challenge produced, not only were there many more unfriendly than friendly Indians in New England, but there was also an eruption in the Indian soul of passionate hatred for the white man and rejection of all his works. They were saying, as eloquently as they knew how, that the invader's civilization was not for them.

Englishmen were often bewildered to discover that the Indian who had been a peaceful neighbor had become a deadly enemy. But what real peace was possible if they were unable to keep out of each other's lives? The Englishman's self-satisfaction with his culture was probably matched by the Indian's self-satisfaction with his. If the English had brought better tools, clothes and food, they were also bearers of new diseases and new vices. It was too early, as yet, for the Indian to feel overwhelmed by the technological superiority of the white civilization. He could see that it was more complex, but why should he not prefer a simpler life with its own joys, subleties and well-ordered government? The English attitude to possessions made no appeal. Literacy aroused no great envy. English ideas about sex were often inconvenient. The English religion was more or less incomprehensible and, striking as it did at the authority of sachems and the validity of the powwow, it was resisted by every tribe that was strong enough to keep it out. Even that pillar of English authority, Massasoit, had upheld—Hubbard reminds us—"the pagan superstition and devilish idolatry"[5] of his tribe.

Between these two unmarriageable ways of life the great burning issues were those of land and sovereignty. The Indian had no concept of private property in land. Land belonged to the tribe. In the name of the tribe the sachem could sell a right to share in the use of the land. The same land could be sold over and over again to as many people as could find room to live, hunt, fish and plant on it. For a time the Indian did not understand that what was being bought from him was not a right of co-occupation but an exclusive ownership. As more and more land was bought, he found he was losing his living-space. He was often cheated in the price of the land and in its boundaries; often betrayed by his own unwary sachems; sometimes overborne by force. It was an unequal, humiliating, infuriating struggle, filled with explosive possibilities.[6]

The claim to sovereignty, asserted with growing pressure on many fronts, eventually produced the war. It was implicit in the subversion of Indian religion and in the settlement of land claims; explicit in the summons of the sachem, the forced surrender of his weapons, and the not uncommon requirement that he buy them back again. It was explicit, too, in the English demand that an Indian should be tried for his offenses in an English court. More important than the question of whether the justice was fairly administered was the question, whose justice? The case of Sassamon, which precipitated the war, illustrates the irreconcilable conflict. From the English standpoint, Sassamon's assailants were fairly tried and convicted of murder by both a jury of white men and an auxiliary jury of Indians. From Philip's standpoint, Sassamon had been guilty of treason, and the Indians who had put him to death had done so under the orders of the tribal authority.[7]

In some collisions between advanced and aboriginal cultures the aboriginal culture may preserve its identity while changing its ways. Was this to be a case where annihilation would be preferred to assimilation?

King Philip's War

Wampanoag Indians never forgot that when the English were weak and the Indians strong, it was Massasoit who had befriended the colonists. No doubt, like Powhatan in Virginia, who helped the Jamestown colonists to stay alive because he looked forward to the help they might give him in dealing with his own tribal enemies, Massasoit's motives were mixed. He was at war with the Narragansetts when the Pilgrims arrived at Plymouth. But whether from hospitality, which was a truly Indian virtue, or from calculation, friendship with the English became the sheet-anchor of his policy. He was at peace with Plymouth Colony from his first mutual defense pact of 1621 up to his death forty years later in 1661. The Narragansett Indians were also persuaded to sign a treaty of peace with the whites who were moving into their territory, and it too would last many years in spite of alarms and tensions.

There was a little incident in 1623 which is worth notice because it contained so many elements of the later tragedies. A group of tough immigrants—"lusty men"—who had been sent over by the London capitalist, John Weston, who financed the Pilgrims, had started a fur-trading station at Wessagusset (Weymouth). The Indians accused the traders of robbery, and the traders accused the Indians of attempted murder. Miles Standish convinced himself that there really was an Indian plot against the English and proceeded with a company from Plymouth to surprise and kill five Indians. When Pastor John Robinson heard of this, he told his erring Pilgrims what he thought of them: "How happy a thing had it been, if you had converted some before you killed any! . . . . You will say they deserved it. I grant it; but by what provocations and invitements by these heathenish Christians (Weston's men) . . . It is also a thing more glorious, in men's eyes, than pleasing in God's or convenient for Christians, to be a terror to poor barbarous people."[8] Pastor Robinson was safe in Holland when he sent this rebuke to his old congregation. Miles Standish had to think of the safety of white men in wilderness America. He also had the help of "friendly" Indians when he struck down the "enemy" Indians.

The only war in New England that preceded Philip's war was the Pequot War of 1637, and this was less a war than a punitive massacre—the kind of police action that becomes a commonplace in the history of colonialism. It began in 1634 when Captain Stone, another dubious furtrader, was killed by the Pequots on the Connecticut River. Under pressure from the English—the Pequots also had their hands full with the Narragansetts—they signed a treaty in Boston agreeing to surrender the murderers, to pay an indemnity, to permit trade, and to allow the settling of Connecticut. Some of these terms were fulfilled, some not. Then two years later another shady Englishman, John Oldham, was murdered by Narragansett Indians on Block Island. The Narragansetts offered amends, but Massachusetts sent an expedition of ninety men under John Endicott to avenge the murder of Oldham and to settle some old scores with the Pequots who were suspected of harboring the murderers of Oldham and who were guilty of the earlier murder of Stone. Issues became thoroughly confused; tempers flared; some good judges, then and since, condemned Endicott as an aggressor; others defended him. The Pequots, stung by English insults and reprisals, tried to get the Narragansetts to join them in war, but found themselves isolated. Miantonomo, the Narragansett chieftain, signed a defense pact with the English in Boston, and Uncas, the Mohegan chieftain who was trying to throw off Pequot suzerainty, teamed up with the English. A combination of English settlers, Narragansett Indians and Mohegan Indians, under the command of Captain Mason, proceeded to deal with the Pequots. It was all on the tiny scale of frontier fighting—Mason commanded less than two hundred men—but they surprised and burnt one of the principal Pequot forts, killing some six or seven hundred Pequots with trifling losses to themselves, and administering a hammerblow which broke the Pequot spirit.

A victory as easy as this led the English to underrate the fighting capacities of the Indian, but it introduced an era of almost forty years in which English sovereignty was asserted without challenge. Power politics among the Indian tribes was dominated by the rivalry between Uncas of the Mohegans, heir to the Pequot power, and the Narragansetts. The United Colonies upheld their protégé, Uncas; agreed to the execution of his captured enemy, the great Miantonomo in 1643; threatened war against the Narragansetts whenever necessary and received their submission. By the middle decades of the century, the English seemed to have found the formula for maintaining a favorable balance of power among the dependent tribes outside their settlements by disciplining first one and then another.

What upset this system was the disappearance of Massasoit from the scene in 1661 and the transformation of the Wampanoags from friends to enemies. Massasoit had introduced his two sons, Wamsutta and Metacomet, to the government of Plymouth before his death. They were given their English names, Alexander and Philip, as a gesture of good will, but the resentment of the younger generation at the encroachments of English power was reflected in both of them. Alexander, called in after his succession to answer charges, died of a fever before he got back home and was suspected—it is believed gratuitously—of being poisoned by the English. Philip cleared himself of suspicion of plotting and renewed his father's covenant with Plymouth as he succeeded his brother in 1662, but he was gradually drawn into resistance. Governor Winslow was going to protest when the war broke out that the Wampanoags had always been fairly treated by Plymouth and it became an article of faith among the English that they were fighting a just war; but what was fair in a good Puritan's eyes could be foul in an Indian's. It was in 1667 that the General Court, with its supply of public land almost exhausted, approved the settlement of Swansea at the mouth of the Mount Hope peninsula on which Philip's village of Sowams was located. No promises of protection could compensate for that sort of proximity.

Philip was next summoned to answer charges of plotting in 1667. If it was hard then to separate fact from rumor, it is impossible now. He protested his innocence; accused his Narragansett enemies of telling lies about him, and was in turn accused. The Plymouth government settled for a contribution of £40 towards the expense of the case and restored his confiscated guns.

Suspected again in 1671, he was called in to Taunton in April and forced to promise that the guns—not just of his retinue but of the tribe—would be surrendered as a pledge of good behavior. A summer of recrimination followed in which Plymouth appealed to her sister colonies and Philip did what he could to win sympathy for his cause among both the English at Boston and such allied tribes as the Sakonnets. But it was a losing game. Awashonks made her peace quickly enough in July; the United Colonies stuck together. Clearly, Philip was in no condition for war. The outcome was an inquest at Plymouth on September 24, 1671, attended by Governor John Leverett of Massachusetts and Governor John Winthrop of Connecticut, as well as by Philip and his counsellors in full regalia. This assembly of notables began as a parley and ended with a conviction. Philip was obliged to scratch his mark at the foot of a new piece of paper, in which he made a full acknowledgment of English authority and accepted a fine of £100.

We shall never know how the resentments of this proud man smoldered in the next three years but we can be sure he made plans for vengeance.

In January 1675 John Sassamon, the Indian who had been first a Christian Indian, then a renegade secretary of Philip, and then again a Christian Indian, warned the Plymouth government that the Wampanoags were organizing a general conspiracy. Soon after, his bludgeoned body was taken out of Assawampsett Pond. Tispaquin, a brother-in-law of Philip, was sachem of Assawampsett. Three Wampanoags, one of them a counsellor of Philip and another, this counsellor's son, were convicted of murder in June, on the testimony of an Indian who swore he had seen them kill Sassamon and push his body beneath the ice. Two of the three went to their deaths protesting their innocence; the third, flung to the ground when the hangman's rope broke, confessed the guilt of his companions. He was the son of the Indian, Tobias, who was Philip's counsellor, and he insisted that he was only an observer of the execution; but his confession did not prevent him from being successfully hanged a month later.

It was this trial and the subsequent hangings which

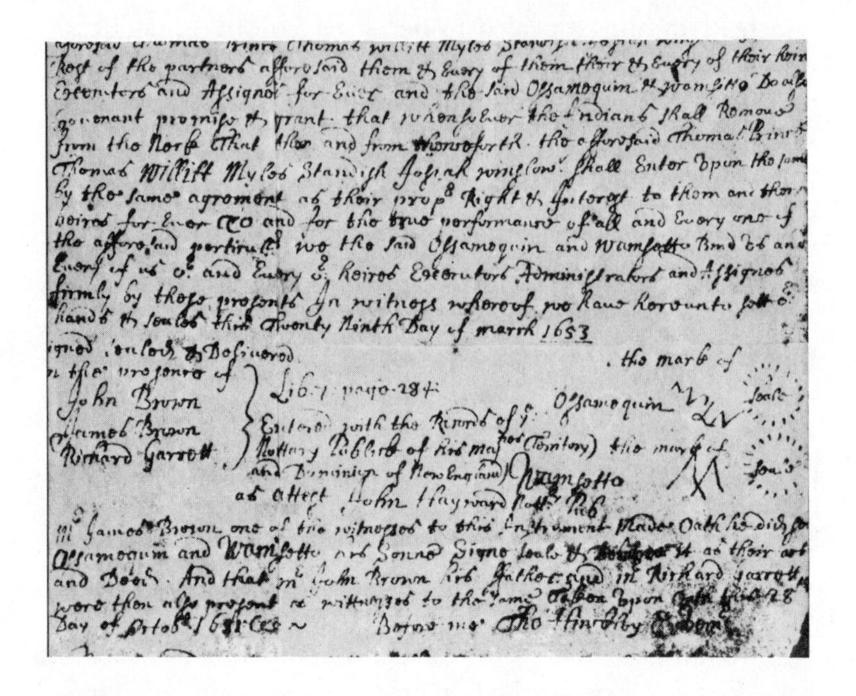

... Thomas Prince Thomas Willitt Myles Standish Josiah ...
Rest of the partners afforesaid them & Every of them their & Every of their heirs
Executors and Assignes for Ever and the said Ossamequin & Wamsitto do also
covenant promise & grant that whensoever the Indians shall Remove
from the Neck that then and from thenceforth the afforesaid Thomas Prince
Thomas Willitt Myles Standish Josiah Winslow shall Enter upon the same
by the same agreement as their prop^r Right & Interest to them and their
heires for Ever To and for the true performance of all and Every one of
the afforesaid particulars wee the said Ossamequin and Wamsitto Bind us and
Every of us o^r and Every o^r heires Executors Administrators and Assignes
firmly by these presents In witness whereof we have hereunto sett o^r
hands & seales this Twenty Ninth Day of march 1653

Signed sealed & Delivered
in the presence of
John Brown
James Brown
Richard Garrett

the mark of
Ossamequin (seale)

Lib 1 page 284
Entered with the Records of ye
Nottary Publick of his Majesties Territory
and Dominion of New England
as attest John Hayward Nott Pub

the mark of
Wamsitto (seale)

Mr James Brown one of the witnesses to this Instrument Made Oath he did see Ossamequin and Wamsitto his sonne Signe seale & deliver it as their act and Deed. And that Mr John Brown his father and Richard Garrett were then also present as witnesses to the same. Taken upon Oath this 28 Day of Octob 1681 etc ~ Before me Tho Hinckley Govr

Deed, with Marks of Massasoit and His Son Wamsutta, March 29, 1653.

Executors and Assignes for ever and the said Ossamequin and Wamsetto do also covenant promise and grant that whenever the Indians shall remove from the neck that then and from thenceforth the afforesaid Thomas Prince Thomas Willitt Myles Standish Josiah Winslow shall enter upon the same by the same agreement as their proper Right and Interest to them and their heires for ever. To and for the true performance of all and every one of the afforesaid particulars we the said Ossamequin and Wamsetto bind us and Every of us our and Every our heires Executors Administrators and Assignes firmly by these presents. In witness whereof we have hereunto sett our hands and seales this twenty-ninth day of March 1653.

Signed Sealed and Delivered
in the presence of:
John Brown
James Brown
Richard Garrett

The mark of

Ossamequin

said neck bounded on the south side by a white oke tree marked on
foure sids standing in a swampe called tompe and so by a eastrely
and a westerly line from the said tree extendin one mile from the sea
side into the woods and from the end of that mile in the woods
northwardly till it meet with a fresh medow in the woods att the
head of pachet brook for the eastwardly bounds and for the
notherly bounds the sd brook called pachet till it meet with the
sea afore said To have and to hold all the above sd tract of
Land with all and singuler the pfits benifits priviledges and
heriditements what so ever with their appurtenances what so-
ever unto the above sd Constant southworth William pabodie
Nathaniel Thomas and their partners as above said and to
every of their heirs and assigns for ever: in witness where of
I the above sd awashunks have here unto set my hand and
seale this one and thirty day of July: one thousand six hundred
seventy three:

Signed sealed and delivered
in the presents of us

Robert Gibbs:

the marke T of John
munros:

the mark: X of awashunks (seal)
and seale

the marke of } potter
the sonn } of awashunks:

potter the son of awashunks appeared before me the
first of November 1673 and freely assented to this
act and deede and also acknowledged his mark as above
before me Will Bradford Assistant

Recorded the 3d of february — 17 12/13
by Nathaniel Searle Clarke:

The First Purchase of Land from Awashonks by the Proprietors of Little Compton, July 31, 1673.

precipitated the war. The Wampanoags sent their squaws across the bay to the safe-keeping of the Narragansetts, while they began their ominous dances. Church tells us how they stirred up the Pocassets and the Sakonnets. Attempts at last-minute peacemaking, by both the Plymouth government and Philip himself, suffered the usual fate. On Sunday, June 20, Philip allowed his braves to storm out of the Mount Hope neck into a raid on the southern fringes of Swansea, where empty houses were looted and burned. On June 23, an English boy shot an Indian looter. The Indians retaliated the next day by killing nine or ten Englishmen, whose mutilated bodies were discovered by some of the would-be peacemakers. War had begun.

A fascinating document has come down to us in which Deputy Governor John Easton, a Rhode Island Quaker, reports an attempt to prevent the war which he and some of his associates had made only a few days before these events. In a visit to Philip they had suggested arbitration, and had mollified his scepticism by proposing that one of the arbitrators might be the Governor of New York and the other a sachem chosen by the Wampanoags themselves. This seems to have struck Philip as a novel idea, and Easton, good Quaker as he was, wished that it might have been tried. But he found himself listening, ineffectually, as they poured out a flood of grievances.

"They said, they had been the first in doing good to the English, and the English the first in doing wrong; when the English first came, the king's father was as a great man, and the English as a little child; he constrained other Indians from wronging the English, and gave them corn and showed them how to plant, and was free to do them any good, and had let them have a hundred times more land than now the king had for his own people. But their king's brother, when he was king, came miserably to die, by being forced to court, as they judge poisoned.

"And another grievance was, if twenty of their honest

Indians testified that an Englishman had done them wrong, it was as nothing; and if but one of their worst Indians testified against any Indian or their king, when it pleased the English, it was sufficient.

"Another grievance was, when their kings sold land, the English would say it was more than they agreed to,[9] and a writing must be proof against all of them; and some of their kings had done wrong to sell so much that they left their people none; and some being given to drunkenness the English made them drunk and then cheated them in bargains. Now their kings were forewarned not to part with land for nothing, in comparison to the value thereof. Those whom the English had owned for king or queen, they would now disinherit and make another king that would give or sell them those lands; so that now they had no hopes left to keep any land.

"Another grievance, the English cattle and horses still increased so that when they removed thirty miles from where the English had anything to do, they could not keep their corn from being spoiled. They never being used to fence, they thought that when the English bought land of them, they would have kept their cattle upon their own land.

"Another grievance, the English were so eager to sell the Indians liquors that most of the Indians spent all in drunkenness and then ravened upon the sober Indians and they did believe often did hurt the English cattle, and their kings could not prevent it.

"We knew before that these were their grand complaints. . . we only endeavoured to persuade them that all complaints might be righted without war, but could have no other answer but that they had not heard of that way for the governor of New York and an Indian king to have the hearing of it. We had cause to think that if that had been tendered it would have been accepted. We endeavored, however, that they should lay down their arms, for the English were too strong for them. They said, 'Then the English should do for them as they did when they were too strong for the English.'

"So we departed without any discourteousness, and suddenly had a letter from the Plymouth governor that they intended in arms to conform Philip, but with no information what they required, nor on what terms he refused to have their quarrel decided. And in a week's time after we had been with the Indians, the war thus began."[10]

An ear tuned to both the idealism and the politics of a Rhode Island point of view at this time will not miss the overtones of this report. But in a larger sense we may ask, "What options did the Indians have?" In the fullness of time it was to become a choice between absorption or annihilation, with a miserable existence on a reservation as the only possible compromise.[11] At this early stage, it was less clear cut. They could accept the status of dependent tribes under English protection with less and less security for their way of life. They could try to assimilate themselves to English ways, in the manner of praying Indian villages, with some sort of future as lower-caste peasants, eked out by agricultural and domestic service for their white masters. They could migrate westwards; in which case they would collide with hostile Indians, and, if they survived these encounters, enjoy a breathing space until English expansion caught up with them again. Or they could take up arms, burning and destroying, until the English were thoroughly chastened, or driven into the sea, or until honor at least was satisfied—a heroic choice, which would have seemed less suicidal at this time than it does to us in retrospect.

One of the great enigmas of King Philip's War is the character and aims of King Philip himself. Was he the author of a grand design or the victim of a desperate muddle? Did he mastermind a confederation or was the spreading combustion as unplanned as brush fires? Was he *the* ringleader or simply *one* of the ringleaders? Was he forced to open the war before he was ready? Was the Indian tradition of warfare an essentially limited one, or did he really dream of a war of annihilation? Did he return to Mount Hope in the summer of 1676 to meet a brooding death or to fight another day?

These various views of his aims have been accompanied by arguments about his courage. Nineteenth-century antiquarians like Samuel Drake and Henry Dexter went to extreme lengths to debunk the romantic Indian-worship of their day. Not only did they deny to Philip any claim to statesmanship or to broad generalship, but they also came close to calling him a coward.[12] They said he never struck a blow in a battle, that anyone ever reported, and was always the first to run away!

His aims and his control of events will always remain a mystery, but it would seem likely that he hoped to harass and unnerve the English by widespread terrorism and did his implacable best to muster the support of other tribes. We know the pressure he put on Weetamoo's Pocassets and Awashonk's Sakonnets. We read in Hubbard how Sagamore John excused himself from his part in the destruction of Brookfield by saying that Philip had forced him into it. Church believed he had gone as far afield as Albany in search of allies. Were the colonists just inventing a bogeyman when they named the war after him and ascribed all sorts of diabolical cunning to him?

One image of Philip which stuck in Church's memory were the words used by the Indian executioner as he quartered his dead body, "he had been a very great man, and had made many a man afraid of him."[13] We should not deprive Philip of his bigness. The charge of cowardice is based on a misconception of his tactics. No one knew better than Church, when he planned the ambush in which Philip was finally trapped and killed, that his arch enemy was "always foremost in the flight." But it never occurred to him to hold that to his discredit.

Indian tactics were not Philip's invention, but he was clearly an expert in them. The essence of Indian warfare was the raid—the stealthy approach, the whirling attack, the hand-to-hand combat in which every man fought for himself. The art was for small parties to keep on the move, ambushing, killing, burning; rarely facing a fight in the open without the benefit of surprise; and melting into the swamps before superior force. The English had everything to learn about this kind of fighting, handicapped as they were by their European manuals, their notions of static warfare, and their forty years of peace. It was Church's genius to teach them all he had discovered from studying the Indian, but even so, they suffered severely. Imagine the feelings of the householder encircled by the forest: "They know where we are! We never know where they are!" The beleaguered settlers evacuated their outlying houses; fortified others as strong points; built palisades; kept a little village force on standing notice; and looked to the government to hunt down the enemy and destroy him in his swamps by commissioning a roving company of the kind that Church led.

The war was a terrifying experience which lasted seventeen months—from June 1675 to October 1676. It goes without saying that during the opening rounds there were the usual numbskulls in the higher command—all those aging incompetents and resolute blockheads with ignominy in their knapsacks! The English leaders were defensive when they should have been aggressive; they diverted forces to bully the Narragansetts into signing a treaty when they should have concentrated on crushing Philip; they pulled companies out of battle areas for unaccountable reasons and struggled ineptly with the problems of supplies. After eluding them in the opening campaign around Mount Hope, Philip eluded them again in Pocasset and then escaped across the Taunton River when they thought they had him pinned down in a swamp.

He was headed westwards for the Nipmuck country, across the Rehoboth plain and the Pawtucket River, when yet another chance to hunt him down was missed at Nipsachuck, twelve miles northwest of Providence, where his pursuers let him get away again.

This was on August 1, 1675, after five weeks of war in which Wampanoags and their satellites had raided Swansea, Rehoboth, Taunton, Middleborough and Dartmouth; a group of Narragansetts had done some damage at Providence; and a party of Nipmucks had attacked Mendon in southern Massachusetts. Philip and his warriors struck off northward to strengthen the pro-war faction among the Nipmucks. Weetamoo and her people branched off southward to join the Narragansetts. The two largest groups of Algonquian Indians were about to be drawn into the war.

Massachusetts had made several attempts to preserve the loyalty of the Nipmucks during these tense weeks. Ordinarily, this tribe was a loose federation of scattered villages, each under its own sachem and often on the best of terms with the English pioneer farmers—indissolubly so, thought the farmers of Brookfield, Springfield, and many another peaceful outpost; but the messengers from Boston found the Nipmuck villages deserted. They had rendezvoused and were offering no encouragement to parley. When the party from Boston persisted in trying to see them, they were ambushed and driven back into the tiny frontier community of Brookfield, which was then besieged, bloodied, relieved by the English, and finally abandoned. This was the kind of history that repeated itself in September and October, with different degrees of terror, up and down the Connecticut River, in Springfield, Hatfield, Bloody Brook, Deerfield and Northfield. Philip cannot be identified in any of these actions, but it is assumed that he was present in either the spirit or the flesh. The burden of the English defenses fell on the forces of Massachusetts and Connecticut; Plymouth took no part in this fighting but it was soon to be involved in another western theatre.

The Narragansetts had been playing a waiting game since the treaty which had been extracted from them on July 15 and confirmed on October 18. Under this engagement, they were supposed to abstain from unfriendly acts and to hand over all the enemy Indians that fell into their hands. Ninigret, sachem of the southern Narragansetts, made a point of handing over Wampanoag scalps because he was counting on an English victory. But other powerful sachems were either neutral or worse. They offered hospitality to the fugitives from Mount Hope or Pocasset, failed to control their young braves, and were thought to be meditating war. Should this formidable tribe be coerced at the risk of enlarging the war? Could the English afford not to try a knockout blow?

The colonists won their first victory of the war at the Great Swamp Fight on December 19, 1675, when the combined forces of all the colonies, under the command of Governor Winslow, fell on the Narragansetts in their winter fort near West Kingston. There may have been a thousand Indians, men, women and children, inside the fort and about the same number—though all of them men—in Winslow's army. A heavy price was paid in English casualties. Seven of the fourteen company commanders died either in the fort or on the next day's cruel march, when the dead and wounded were carried back to Wickford through the snow. The Indian casualties were far higher, but it was not the annihilating victory which Commander Winslow had hoped for. It was a month before the Narragansett warriors were chased out of their territory into the Nipmuck country, and no other decisive action had been fought by February 5, when Winslow was obliged to disband his forces.

From February to May 1676, the tide of Indian raids was almost unchecked by any English success. If we can see clearly today that time was on the English side, there was very little comfort during these months for the exposed settlements.

Nipmucks, Wampanoags, and now Narragansetts were encamped in the wilderness between the frontier towns of the Boston area and those on the upper Connecticut River. Most of the Nipmucks were near Menamset or Mount Wachusett. Some were near Brookfield, where Philip had been seen upon his return from Albany, after a search for allies among the Mohawks. The devastating attacks on the outer ring of the Boston area began in February. Town after town—Lancaster, Medfield, Groton, Marlborough, Wrenthan, Sudbury—endured its ordeal. While Nipmucks inflicted these damages, Wampanoags and Narragansetts made their way back into Plymouth Colony and Rhode Island to wreak destruction on Rehoboth, Providence, Bridgewater, and other outposts. Alarms were sounded at points as widely scattered as Weymouth and Scituate on the coast, Andover and Chelmsford on the north, Northampton and Springfield in the west.

It was not until April and May that the attacks showed signs of faltering. A Connecticut force of Englishmen, Pequots, Mohegans, and Niantics made a successful raid into the Narragansett country, where Canonchet, son of Miantonomo, was caught on a trip he was making to a secret hiding place for seed corn. This luckless hero, aflame with pride, was executed at Stonington in the early days of April by the Mohegans who had killed his father a generation before; Uncas' brother had hatcheted Miantonomo; Uncas' son shot Canonchet.

Another force from Hatfield, Hadley and Northampton disrupted the Indians who were fishing at the falls of the Connecticut River above Deerfield. Disease broke out among tribes weakened by hunger. A Providence man writing to England told how some enemy Indians were killing their children because the noise of their crying betrayed them and they had no food left for them.[14] The prospect of a second year of hiding in forests and swamps away from their agricultural area filled more and more Indians with desperation. Hubbard believed that many of the confederates lost hope at this time, blaming Philip for the losses he had brought upon them, making their way back to their own areas, and putting out feelers for peace.

Plans for the June campaigns were now made by the United Colonies. The combined expedition of Massachusetts and Connecticut forces, which rendezvoused at Hadley and combed the Connecticut River as far north as Northfield, returned empty-handed; but the Connecticut contingent then inflicted smashing defeats on the Narragansetts who had gone back to their own territory. The old squaw, Quaiapen, was killed in the battle at Nipsachuck on July 20. Benjamin Church, who had come out of his retirement on the island, was arranging the submission of Awashonks and the Sakonnets in June and July. A Plymouth exped-dition, under Major Bradford, was organized to patrol Philip's old haunts in the Swansea, Rehoboth, Taunton triangle. Church was then given a commission to raise a company of English and Indians, which began an amazing series of successes in the same area. It became clear that King Philip's War was about to end where it had begun.

While parties of half-starved, disheartened Indians were surrendering all over New England, the chiefs who were beyond hope or thought of mercy were killed or captured one by one. Pumham, one of the toughest of the Narragansett sachems, was killed at Mendon on July 25, and his son captured. Matoonas, the Nipmuck sachem who had originally sacked Mendon, was handed over at Boston on July 27 by Sagamore John, his betrayer, who then shot him on the Boston Common at the order of the English authorities. Unkompoin, Philip's uncle, was killed in a skirmish near the Taunton River on August 1. Philip's wife and their little son were captured by Church on the same day. Weetamoo, Philip's sister-in-law, after escaping capture on August 6, was drowned in the Taunton River in a desperate effort to get back to her own country. Her Narragansett husband,

Quinnapin, Canonchet's cousin, was to be executed in Newport on August 25. The end came for Philip on August 12 and for Annawon, his last great captain, on September 11.

We keep forgetting how small was the scale of this warfare. King Philip may have had three hundred fighting men in his tribe at Mount Hope. The height of Church's ambition was to command a mixed company of two hundred to three hundred English and Indians; he pulled off many of his feats with patrols of twenty to forty. The biggest assemblage of force that any contemporary ever mentioned — and they exaggerated, as we all do in war—was a thousand men. But if the armies were small, so was the scale of life. We have some idea of the suffering when we realize that about a dozen English towns were utterly destroyed and forty others more or less damaged. Some six to eight hundred Englishmen may have been killed—a heavier loss, proportionately, than Americans have endured in any subsequent war. The losses for the Indians were trifling in property, altogether heavier in lives, and murderous to the spirit.

The war fanned every prejudice which fear and hatred could produce. No English description was too bad to do justice to the treachery and cruelty of the Indians and the Indian vocabulary was no doubt equally strained by the description of English vices. Praying Indians were caught in the middle. Hysteria forced Boston to intern her praying Indians on Deer Island, where they were often threatened with violence. Enemy Indians avenged themselves on Christian Indians. Neither side shrank from atrocities.

When it was over, it became clear that Indians in New England were a dying race. They had made a final, heroic, passionate, futile bid for survival with self-respect. Although communities survived, like the groups at Little Compton and Dartmouth that fought for Church in his later expeditions, rum, pestilence, and a failure of heart kept reducing their numbers.[15] Eliot's vision of a Christianized, civilized, Anglicized Indian had evaporated.

The surrender of Philip's regalia to Benjamin Church by the great Annawon, who had served both Philip and his father Massasoit, marked the real end of these Algonquian Indians. Compared with the standards of literate peoples, who have dramatized or philosophized about their defeats, this was a stoical, inarticulate passing. But it has its own heart-clutching eloquence. If Annawon moves us by his dignity in defeat, the death of "the famous Totoson" is beyond tears. With his family, his last son, and all hope destroyed, "his heart became as a stone within him, and he died. The old squaw flung a few leaves and a brush over him and came into Sandwich, and gave this account of his death, and offered to show them where she left his body; but never had the opportunity, for she immediately fell sick and died also."

Benjamin Church

Benjamin Church was born at Plymouth in 1639. His father, Richard Church, had probably come over from England in the fleet which brought Governor Winthrop, and the founders of the Massachusetts Bay Colony, to Boston in 1629. Richard Church settled in Plymouth in 1630 and married Elizabeth Warren in 1636. He was a carpenter who helped to build the first meeting-house in Plymouth. He also saw service as a sergeant in the Pequot War of 1637 and may well have had something to tell the future Indian fighter about Indian warfare. He raised at least nine children and was living in Hingham when he died in 1668.

Benjamin was brought up in his father's trade. We know nothing about his early life until we learn that he married Alice Southworth, daughter of Constant and Elizabeth Southworth, of Duxbury. This was a year before his father died, when he was about twenty-seven, and she about twenty-one. His father-in-law was a person of standing at Plymouth, whose mother had become the second wife of Governor Bradford and who had held the offices of deputy and treasurer for many years. He was to be the Commissary-General of the little colony in King Philip's War.

It was in Duxbury that Benjamin Church joined the company that was formed to settle the lands at Sakonnet and to found the town that became in due course Little Compton. Writing from memory at the end of his life, he begins his memoirs by telling how he was captivated by the sight of this place when he was persuaded to inspect it in 1674 by another enthusiast, Captain John Almy of Rhode Island. But he forgets to mention that he had bought up some rights in this land a year or so earlier, from the indentured servants to whom it had been assigned by Plymouth Colony. The twenty-nine original Proprietors included his

The John Alden House at Duxbury, Mass., where William Pabodie, a Proprietor of Little Compton, Married Betty Alden.

father-in-law, Constant Southworth, his brother, Joseph Church, and no doubt other relatives as well. There is a John Irish among the Proprietors, and we know that one of Church's sisters-in-law married an Irish.

The Proprietors authorized his father-in-law, together with William Pabodie and Nathaniel Thompson, to act as an executive committee that would buy out the rights of the Indians. Seventy-five pounds was paid to Awashonks, squaw-sachem of the Sakonnet Indians, on July 31, 1673, for land which ran southwards from Pachet Brook on the north to a landing place called Toothos (the present Taylor's Lane) and a white oak tree in Tompe Swamp (the present Wilbour Woods). On April 10, 1674, the company met at Duxbury to draw lots for the 32 shares into which the land had been divided. Benjamin drew lots Nos. 19 and 29 and began to clear and develop No. 19 on what is now the south side of Windmill Hill. He tells us in his Foreword, "I was the first Englishman that built upon that neck, which was full of Indians."[16]

In the years that followed King Philip's War—he was thirty-seven when it finished—he lived up to his own image of himself as "a person of uncommon activity and industry."[17] He bought and sold lands, cleared and built on them, cut roads throught the wilderness, founded new plantations, established churches and schools, and shared in the government of his town and colony. In the late seventies he was developing lands in Pocasset. In the eighties and nineties he was one of the founding fathers of Bristol, in Philip's old territory, and made it his home for some fifteen years. By 1697, he had moved on to Fall River, where he owned lands and a mill. The Captain Church of King Philip's War, and the Major Church of the first four Eastern Expeditions became the Colonel Church of the Fifth Expedition in 1704. It was probably after this campaign that he returned to his first love, Little Compton, to end his days there. A tablet on the West Main Road marks the site of his last home, near the house, still standing, which his son Thomas built for himself.

We can trace his civic responsibilities from constable to deputy, as he moved from place to place. He was a constable at Duxbury in 1671; a juryman at Plymouth; a magistrate for Sakonnet and Pocasset; a selectman, magistrate, assessor, moderator of the town meeting, founder of the Congregational Church and deputy for Bristol; magistrate, moderator, founder of the Congregational Church and deputy for Little Compton.

Traces of his ties with Indians after the war can be found in the colony records as well as in his memoirs. In November 1676, his promise to a group of Indians that they could stay in the colony and not be sold into slavery was confirmed by the Plymouth court. The next January the court gave eight of his Indian soldiers permission to settle on his lands in Little Compton in return for military service—an almost feudal arrangement! In 1709, he was exchanging lands in Little Compton to accommodate Indians. When he came to write his memoirs, he reported with obvious pleasure that his friendship with the Indians in Little Compton had been "maintained between them to this day."[18]

The story of his death was told in the second edition of his memoirs (1772), which Ezra Stiles edited with the help of information supplied by his descendants.

"The morning before his death, he went about two miles on horseback to visit his only sister, Mrs. Irish, to sympathize with her on the death of her only child. After a friendly and pious visit, in a moving and affecting manner, he took his leave of her, and said, 'It was a last farewell; telling her, he was persuaded he should never see her more; but hoped to meet her in heaven.' Returning homeward, he had not rode above half a mile before his horse stumbled, and threw him over his head: and the colonel being exceeding fat and heavy, fell with such force that a blood vessel was broken, and the blood gushed out of his mouth like a

Ruins of Benjamin Church's House at Bristol, R. I., circa 1880.

Benjamin Church's Sword.

torrent. His wife was soon brought to him; he tried but was unable to speak to her, and died in about twelve hours. He was carried to the grave in great funeral pomp, and was buried under arms, and with military honours."[19]

His tombstone in the graveyard at Little Compton is inscribed, "Here lyeth interred the [body] of the Honourable Col. BENJAMIN CHURCH, Esq. who departed this life, January 17, 1717/8 in the 78 yeare of his age."

His reputation in New England at that time had been summed up by Cotton Mather who said that his achievements in King Philip's War were so extraordinary "my reader will suspect me to be transcribing the silly old romances, where the knights do conquer so many giants, if I should proceed unto the particular commemoration of them."[20]

The usual inventory of his possessions and furnishings at his house was taken on February 5, 1718. He had called it "the little farm" and had deeded its 120 acres, with other lands, to his eldest son Thomas, of Bristol, who had helped him to compile his memoirs. The value of the various items amounted to £750-17-0. His sword and belt were listed first, at £ 5. There were two guns valued at £ 3. "Sundry books" accounted for £ 2. Did they include Hubbard's or Mather's histories of Philip's War, with their accounts of his own exploits? Gold rings and buttons, and his silver, came to about £ 30; pewter about £ 7; brass about the same. Three beds, with their curtains, pillows, blankets and fourteen pairs of sheets amounted to over £ 70. Provisions—salt, barrels of beef and pork, cheese, butter, barley, oats, beans, Indian corn and cider—£ 27. Stock—nine cows, four heifers, a pair of oxen, a pair of steers, a bull, seven two-year-old cattle, ten yearling cattle, a score of sheep, five swine, and three horses—about £ 200. A Negro couple, with their clothing and bedding, were valued at £ 100; a servant boy at £ 10; and one, John Tomlin, at £ 3. The inventory also included 138 acres of land in Tiverton, valued at £ 180, which was sold by the family to discharge the Colonel's debts and funeral expenses.[21]

He was survived by his widow, Alice, who had almost died a dozen times when he had departed for what looked like a certain death. He left seven children, for whom he had made various provisions. Thomas, the eldest, had been given houses and lands in Bristol and Little Compton. Edward got a house and lands in Bristol. He became an auctioneer in Boston and it was his son Benjamin, also an auctioneer, who interested himself in the second edition of his grandfather's memoirs, and was the father of Dr. Benjamin Church, a Tory in the American Revolution. The Colonel's daughter, Elizabeth, got lands in Bristol and Freetown. His son, Charles, who became high sheriff of his county and a deputy in the colony court, was given lands in Little Compton—that lot No. 19, on which his father had built his first house in 1674, and the adjoining lot, No. 18, which he had bought in 1688. His son Constant inherited mills in Tiverton and lands in Freetown. There was also an unmarried son Benjamin and a daughter, Martha, but there is no record of deeds to them.

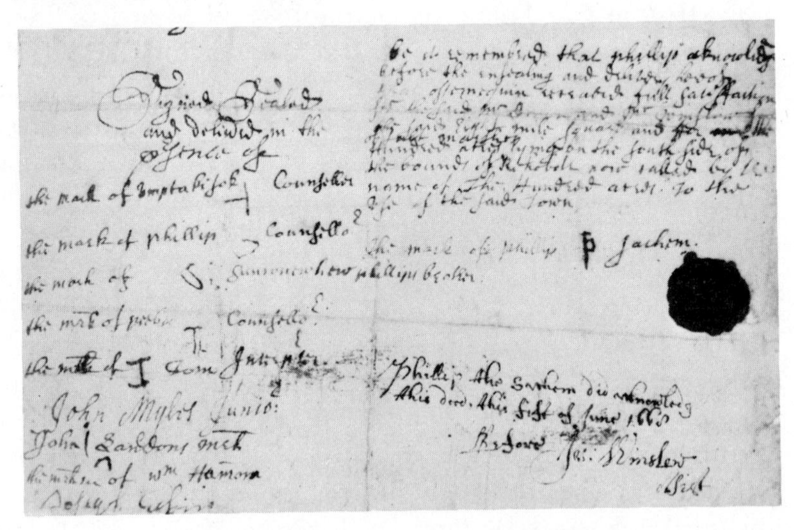
Be it remembered that phillip acknowledg[illegible] before the ensealing and delivery hereof [illegible] full satisfaction [illegible]

Signed Sealed and delivered in the presence of

the mark of [illegible] Counsellor

the mark of phillip Counsellor

the mark of [illegible] phillips brother

the mark of [illegible] Counsellor

the mark of Tom Interpreter

John Myles Junior

the mark of [illegible]

the mark of phillip Sachem.

Philip the Sachem did acknowledge this deed this sixth of June 1668

Before [illegible] Winslow

King Philip's Mark on a Deed of 1668.

His family is represented in Little Compton today by Mr. Carlton Brownell, a direct descendant, and by members of the Burchard family, Mr. John Church Burchard, Mrs. Richard C. Whitin, and Mrs. Paul F. Perkins, who descend from his brother Joseph. Other descendants, Mrs. Ralph Church, Mrs. Jane Dwyer and Mrs. Moosup, Hezekiah Church and Betty Church Chase live in the Bristol neighborhood.

Evolution of a Colonial Classic

It was in his old age that the Colonel turned author. All that we know about the composition of the memoirs is found in his Foreword "To the Reader." He says that he had kept records, which he calls, "my minutes," and that he had solemnly promised to publish some day "the repeated favours of God to myself and those with me in the service." He took up the task when he was too old to serve in the militia—presumably when he was over seventy and settled in his Little Compton home. He described his method of composition in the following words "having my minutes by me, my son has taken the care and pains to collect from them the ensuing narrative of many passages relating to the former and later wars, which I have had the perusal of, and find nothing amiss as to the truth of it, and with as little reflection upon any particular person as might be, either alive or dead."[22]

Ezra Stiles, the editor of the second edition who was in touch with family tradition, described Thomas ambiguously, as "the author or publisher of this history." Church's most meticulous editor, Henry Martyn Dexter, inferred that Benjamin dictated the memoirs to Thomas. He may have done so; but we have really no idea of how the labor of composition was divided between father and son, or in what state his "minutes" were. His records obviously included the commissions and letters which make up so much of his narrative of the Eastern Expeditions—the second part of his memoirs which is not included here. But did they also include journals and memoranda which he had kept at the time, or is all the detail of his adventures in King Philip's War still sharp in his mind after forty years?[23] It is tempting to think that there must have been memoranda, and it is interesting to stumble on a statement in his memoirs about his examination of an Indian—"which was all minuted down"[24]—that shows us he was in the habit of taking notes in the field.

Whatever Thomas's role may have been, as secretary under supervision, we can easily believe that the style of the memoirs bears the stamp of the Colonel's character. Behind the courtesies and restraints lies the dispraise of a strong, simple, shrewd, self-made soldier for the stupidity of military commanders and the ingratitude of governments. If they had taken his advice, the war would have been won sooner and with less sacrifice! There would also have been a better peace if the lives of great Indian captains like Annawon had been spared! "In victory, magnanimity" made as much sense to this village hero as to many an imperial statesman.

Later editors and catalogers have labeled the story which father and son put together, "Church's History of Philip's War," but we can be sure that neither of them thought of it in those terms. They were recording for posterity the memoirs of an old soldier—"telling of the many ran-counters he has had and yet is come off alive!"[25]—who had much to be proud of and thankful for. They were Puritans, living among ministers and elders who made a literary genre out of the records of "remarkable providences." They felt that they had a very exciting story to tell, and a

Entertaining Paſſages
Relating to
Philip's WAR
WHICH
Began in the Month of *June*, 1 6 7 5.
AS ALSO OF
EXPEDITIONS
More lately made
Againſt the Common Enemy, and *Indian* Rebels,
in the Eaſtern Parts of *New-England*:
WITH
Some Account of the Divine Providence
TOWARDS
Benj. Church Eſqr;

By *T. C.*

BOSTON: Printed by *B. Green*, in the Year, 1 7 1 6.

Title Page of First Edition of Church's Diary, 1716.

religious duty to tell it. In this spirit, the first edition of 1716, printed by B. Green in Boston, carries their own accurate title—though a little long for modern taste; "Entertaining Passages relating to Philip's War which Began in the Month of June 1675. As also of Expeditions more lately Made against the Common Enemy, and Indian Rebels in the Eastern Parts of New England: with Some Account of the Divine Providence towards Benj. Church Esq; by T. C."[26]. A modern reader who might be shocked at the use of the word "entertaining" in the title of a war-diary should remember that in the history of the English language "entertaining" meant "interesting" before it meant "amusing."

It was a slender little quarto of 120 pages, with a densely printed page. The only explanatory material was the Foreword "To the Reader." There were no notes or illustrations. It ends so abruptly that Henry Martyn Dexter wondered whether the printer, who was cramming words onto his last page to avoid using another, had not chopped off a sentence or two!

Over half a century later the second edition was published by Solomon Southwick at Newport, Rhode Island. It was a small octavo of 199 pages. The editor was Ezra Stiles, then pastor of the Second Congregational Church in Newport and later the president of Yale University. His diary reads as follows:

"1771. Dec. 18 . . . Correcting the press for Col. Church's Hist. of K. Philip's War in 1675.

"1771. Dec. 19 . . . Reviewing Col. Benj. Church's History of K. Philip's War, 1676, at the request of the printer;—adding English or present Names of places written in Indian names in the Original. Mr. Southwick is printing a Second Edition: first Edit. 1718 [*sic*].

"1772. Apr. 9 . . . Finished writing the Life of Col. Benjamin Church, to be affixed to the new Edition of his

History of the Indian war, called K. Philip's War, now printing. He was born 1639, and died at Little Compton, Janry. 1717/8, *Aet.* 78.

"1772. Apr. 10 . . . Inspecting the Press."[27]

Ezra Stiles was an intellectual magpie, forever stuffing his notebooks with facts and ideas that caught his fancy. When he went to Newport at the age of 28, in 1755, he was already an insatiable collector of Indian lore—their dwindling numbers, their dwellings, their religion, their sexual habits, their supposed origins as one of the lost tribes of Israel. Notebook in hand on all his wanderings, he interrogated Indians, counted them, measured and sketched their wigwams, jotted down Indian names, dug up Indian bones on the scene of the Great Swamp Fight, copied entries out of old books and wrote avidly for the latest information about Indians from correspondents in the west.[28] Too busy gathering material ever to get a book of his own published, he must have been easily persuaded to bring out a new edition of Church. The suggestion may have come from his neighbor, the Newport printer, or from Benjamin Church, a grandson of the Colonel now nearing seventy, who supplied him with biographical information and a Latin ode.[29]

Stiles gave the title of the first edition a nudge towards its modern form by changing "Entertaining Passages" to "Entertaining History." He included a brief life of the Colonel and two engravings by Paul Revere, one of Benjamin Church, the other of King Philip. No examination of Stiles's voluminous papers in the Yale University Library has yet uncovered any reference to these engravings—either how they were commissioned or how they were executed—and each has achieved its own celebrity as a picture which Revere concocted from other sources. This business-like plagiarism was not at all unusual in his day, but a nineteenth-century editor like Samuel Drake took it for granted that the picture of Church was an original like-

THE

ENTERTAINING

HISTORY

OF

King *Philip*'s WAR,

Which began in the Month of *June*, 1675.

AS ALSO OF

EXPEDITIONS

MORE LATELY MADE

Againſt the Common Enemy, and *Indian* Rebels, in the Eaſtern Parts of *New-England* :

With ſome ACCOUNT of the Divine Providence towards

Col. Benjamin Church:

BY THOMAS CHURCH, ESQ. HIS SON.

THE SECOND EDITION.

BOSTON: Printed, 1716.

NEWPORT, *Rhode-Iſland*: Reprinted and Sold by SOLOMON SOUTHWICK, in *Queen-Street*, 1772.

(Left) Title Page of Second Edition, 1772. (Above) Portrait of Ezra Stiles, Editor of Second Edition.

Model for Revere's Engraving of King Philip.

Revere's Engraving of King Philip.

ness until Charles Deane voiced his suspicions in 1858. By 1882, Deane had demonstrated that the engraving of Church was an exact copy of an engraving of the English poet, Charles Churchill, which had appeared in an English magazine of 1768, the only difference being that Revere had slung a powder horn around the poet's neck. Not unnaturally many people, including Deane himself, have concluded that there was no resemblance whatever between Churchill and Church. But, of course, there may have been! Dexter suggested, with his usual acuteness, that Church's grandson might have remembered his grandfather's face, and might have approved Revere's model for that reason. We know that the young Benjamin lived in or around the old Benjamin's home until he was eleven. Dexter goes on to say that he was strengthened in this guesswork by the way in which the descendants of Church whom he himself had met looked very like Charles Churchill![30]

But there was no grandson of Philip to protect his interests. Revere's Philip has been called ugly, grim, grotesque, a terror to children. It reminds us that whereas the seventeenth century often had a wholesome fear of the Indian, and the nineteenth century often romanticized him, the eighteenth century as often despised him. Though this neurotic pygmy could never have been anything other than Revere's fantasy, it was left to Bradford Swan to demonstrate in 1959, with wit and precision, where the artist had borrowed his ideas.[31] Three different engravings were involved: two were of Mohawk chiefs—hardly a model that Philip, their tribal enemy, would have relished!—who had visited Queen Anne in 1710 and had been painted for her by John Verelst; the third was an English print of a group of Ohio Indians. But Revere must also have read his Church, for the decorative detail which he put on Philip's wampum could only have been suggested by Church's description of Philip's regalia.[32]

After the passage of another half-century, Southwick's

edition of 1772 fell into the hands of a young man with a passion for history and an eye for an opportunity as an editor, publisher and bookseller—Samuel Gardner Drake. When he was 32 he opened the first antiquarian bookstore in America and made it a resort for literary Boston. He devoted his life to rescuing all the memorials he could find of the founders of New England, launched the *New England Historical and Genealogical Register,* and left a library of over 15,000 books and 30,000 pamphlets on American history. He was 26 when he stumbled on Church's story. Delighted by it, and convinced it would sell, he got a thousand subscribers and sold out his edition in three months with a net profit of about $500. He never found a copy of the first edition of 1716, which by his day was a very rare book. His edition, which we may call the third, was a reprint of the second, with a greatly enlarged editorial apparatus. It came out in 1825, in a duodecimo of 304 pages, printed by Howe and Norton, at 14 State Street, Boston. Though Drake, as he explained later, was only just getting to know his subject, he included an index, some footnotes, a more flattering picture of King Philip, which a Providence engraver foisted on him,[33] and a forty-page appendix on early New England history.

The public was obviously ready for more. Ancestor-worship, romantic interest in the Indian, and a growing concern for sound scholarship was multiplying readers. Drake brought out a second and bigger edition of his first work in 1827—the same text with more footnotes, newly engraved copies of Revere's portraits, more illustrations, a larger appendix, 360 pages in all. The plates of this popular work were bought by different printers in New England and used repeatedly over the next two decades. The illustrations may differ, but the texts are all re-issues of the edition of 1827, with only the slightest changes.[34]

Samuel Drake is a respected name among lovers of Colonial history. He published all the contemporary accounts of King Philip's War he could discover, gave us editions of William Hubbard's and Increase Mather's histories, and put out book after book about the Indian. He was an infectious enthusiast who became a grand old man of learning in American and Indian history. But as an editor of Church, he has to yield to Henry Martyn Dexter, the perfect model of scrupulous, indefatigable scholarship.

Revere's Engraving of Benjamin Church (1772) and His Model, Mr. Charles Churchill.

Buried in every first-class antiquarian is a boy's curiosity. Dexter's imagination had been fired as a boy by the story of Church's campaigns. He knew every inch of the ground and made it his business to ferret out every accessible fact. He found a copy of the rare first edition of 1716, which had eluded Drake, and pounced like a hawk on the few errors which had been made by Southwick and Stiles in 1772 and then unwittingly perpetuated by Drake. In his own edition, which is the fifth according to our reckoning, he reproduced the text of the first edition, with minute exactitude, down to the smallest typographical errors, in a modern antique type which came as close to the original as possible. A page of Dexter's text is cleaner and more elegant than the first edition, because it is better printed, on better paper, with eleven words to a line as compared with fourteen, and twenty-eight lines to a full page as compared with forty-two. He reviews the previous editions; provides materials for a life of Church by summarizing the entries in the Colonial records; supplies an introduction to the wars, two good maps, a chronology of events, and a stately promenade of footnotes—topographical, genealogical and historical—which occupy, on the average, at least half of each page of text.

Dexter's first volume, containing the first part of the memoirs which deals with King Philip's War, came out in 1865. His second volume, containing the second part which covers the five Eastern Expeditions between 1689 and 1704, appeared in 1867. John Kimball Wiggin, of Boston, was the printer of this beautiful edition, which consisted of no more that 250 copies, small quarto, and 35 copies, royal quarto. Dexter's dedication, to the most respected historian of his day, tells us something about both the author and his age.

"To John Gorham Palfrey, D.D., L.L.D., who adds the minute and patient accuracy of the antiquary to the broad and philosophical insight of the historian; and who has, more faithfully than any other writer, conceived and defined the real position occupied by the aborigines of New England in the civil and social scale; this edition of a homely but invaluable tract, having large reference to them, is, by permission, most respectfully inscribed."

God bless the Dexters of the antiquarian world! His edition of Church will always be the scholar's choice, and any new edition, such as this one, must lean heavily on him. A comparison of his text with the text of the first edition reveals no mistakes, except those which he faithfully copied. Modern scholarship has added much to our general understanding of King Philip's War, as we can see from an admirable study like Douglas Leach's *Flintlock and Tomahawk* which appeared in 1958, but very little to what Dexter knew about Church and his story.

(Left) Engraving of King Philip from Drake's Edition of 1825.
(Right) Portrait of Samuel Drake, Editor of the "Third" and "Fourth" Editions.

This sixth edition of ours coincides with another chapter in the evolution of a Colonial classic. If there are few new facts about Church and his narrative, there is a surge of interest in relations between red men and white men which is producing a new realism and a new romanticism in historical interpretation. The concept of the Indian as "savage" was never in worse disrepute than it is today. Anthropologists and archaeologists have steadily advanced our capacity to understand the Indian's culture in its own terms and the dynamics of the interaction between his culture and ours. The re-thinking and re-writing of black history in the past decade has stimulated a desire to re-think and re-write red history. Ignorance of Christianity and scepticism about its missionaries has made it tempting to see nothing but racism in a Puritan mission. And a civilization which is racked by a sense of guilt and anxiety whenever it contemplates its polluted, depleted environment, feels a new nostalgia for the so-called "savage" who seems to have lived at peace with his. At no time since the romantic idolization of the Indian in the early nineteenth century has his Puritan conqueror received such a withering press.

In this volume we reproduce the text which Dexter used with slight modifications in the interests of the contemporary reader. We have eliminated the long-tailed *s*; modernized much of the spelling and punctuation and have taken the liberty of breaking up some of the long paragraphs which, in some cases, run on for pages in the original. We have also introduced subheads in a type clearly distinguishable from the text. We have left the proper names and place names exactly as Church spelled them.

Evaluation

How interesting are these memoirs?

They tell a good story, which is another way of saying that they are interesting as literature. Church was not able to live up to these standards when he undertook the second part of these memoirs which deals with his five Eastern Expeditions in the years between 1689 and 1704. There are

Portrait of Henry Martyn Dexter, Editor of the "Fifth Edition.

flashes of the old spirit, but there are also dull retreats into official records. Maine was strange country. The Indians there—how unlike Awashonks, or Philip, or Annawon!—were anonymous. They were much harder to bring to battle. And he was much more the administrator, carrying the burdens of commander-in-chief, than the captain of a company, foraging on his own, and watching his Indians scamper off like horses, at his bidding.[35] His old man's memory kindles into flame when he thinks of his first commands, then fumbles in smoke over the officialdom and frustrations of the later years. How much harder to breathe life into all those commissions which lie among his "minutes." He must have said to himself, as he looked out of his farm windows on to the Sakonnet River, "Let Thomas print them as he finds them!"

But the first part is one of the great adventure stories of Colonial America, with a hero whose capacity for courage, endurance, initiative and simplicity of heart captivates his readers.

These memoirs also rate very highly as history. Some such thought was in his mind when he wrote in his Foreword: "seeing every particle of historical truth is precious, I hope the reader will pass a favorable censure upon an old soldier telling of the many ran-counters he has had."[36] How many guerilla fighters have written their memoirs? Not a few, perhaps. But how many have described the first great Indian war in American history? This is eye-witness history, by the ablest fighter on the English side—"a person of great loyalty and the most successful of our commanders,"[37] said Governor Winslow to King Charles II, when he sent him Philip's regalia, which Annawon had surrendered to Church.

The Reverend William Hubbard put together a good story of this war, of the sort that a learned, conscientious clergyman might write in an age which expected journalism from its clergy. He published it immediately. Increase Mather, with the same instinct for his public, kept a journal

A Nineteenth Century Engraving of King Philip.

which saw the light of day as soon. These were professional writers; but they were never grazed by a bullet. There were other Bostonians who got into print as quickly as possible, like Nathaniel Saltonstall and Richard Hutchinson, but with no more authority than is now needed to sell a piece to a magazine. Much closer to Church were the soldiers of his day, whose reports were published by Boston's only printer or circulated in manuscript. Thomas Wheeler wrote a story during the war with a title which is in the same style that Church used for his own memoirs: *"A True Narrative of the Lord's Providences in Various Dispensations towards Captain Edward Hutchinson of Boston and Myself, and Those that Went with Us into the Nipmuck Country."*[38] Major Walley, who persuaded Church to undertake the Eastern Expedition of 1692, published a narrative of the Quebec expedition of 1690;[39] Colonel Hathorne, who superseded Church in the Eastern Expedition of 1696, was another soldier who wrote a journal. Church makes it clear that he had read Hathorne's work,[40] it would be odd if he had not read, or heard about, Walley's. But his memoirs outstrip all of these. Each might have said, if put in competition with Church, what Captain Bradford once wrote when he and Church set off in search of Philip's headquarters, "I shall not put myself out of breath to get before Ben Church!"[41]

This is partly because he was a bigger actor on a larger stage. It is also because he undertook a much more ambitious narrative which has met the tests of accuracy to a very impressive degree, when we remember that it was compiled years after the event it describes.[42] Dexter draws attention to his occasional confusions in chronology, but the amazing thing is how consistent his narrative is both with the histories of Hubbard and Mather and with the field reports which he himself submitted at the time.[43] Finally, there is the light which he sheds on the tactics of fighting with In-

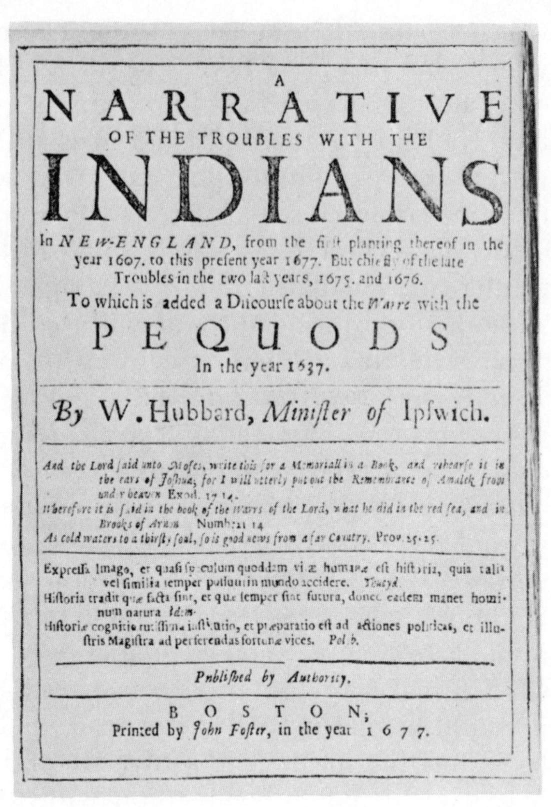

A
NARRATIVE
OF THE TROUBLES WITH THE
INDIANS
In NEW-ENGLAND, from the first planting thereof in the year 1607. to this present year 1677. But chiefly of the late Troubles in the two last years, 1675. and 1676.
To which is added a Discourse about the Warre with the
PEQUODS
In the year 1637.

By W. Hubbard, Miniſter of Ipſwich.

And the Lord ſaid unto Moſes, write this for a Memoriall in a Book, and rehearſe it in the ears of Joſhua; for I will utterly put out the Remembrance of Amalek from under heaven Exod. 17 14.
Wherefore it is ſaid in the book of the Warrs of the Lord, what he did in the red ſea, and in Brooks of Arnon Numb. 21 14
As cold waters to a thirſty ſoul, ſo is good news from a far Country. Prov. 25. 25.

Expreſſa Imago, et quaſi ſpeculum quoddam vitæ humanæ eſt hiſtoria, quia talia vel ſimilia ſemper poſſunt in mundo accidere. *Thucyd.*
Hiſtoria tradit quæ facta ſint, et quæ ſemper ſint futura, donec eadem manet hominum natura. *Idem.*
Hiſtoriæ cognitio rectiſſima inſtitutio, et præparatio eſt ad actiones politicas, et illuſtris Magiſtra ad perferendas fortunæ vices. *Polyb.*

Publiſhed by Authority.

BOSTON;
Printed by *John Foſter*, in the year 1677.

Title Page of William Hubbard's Contemporary History of King Philip's War.

dians, whether as enemies or friends. This puts his memoirs as military history in a class by themselves. He is also an important source for the ethno-historian—his description of the dance on the shore of Mattapoisett, where the chiefs of Awashonk's tribe "made soldiers for him", is a unique record in the seventeenth century literature.[44]

But—to return to the theme from which this Introduction began—what sort of commentary do his memoirs provide on the collision of cultures? What did he think of the Indian? How far behind had he looked? What sort of future did he foresee? Is there any historical perspective? Any philosophy?

To expect history or philosophy from an unread man of action is a little unreal. Church could make a bow in the best company, but he says nothing to suggest that he had ever read a book, except the Bible. And what if he had? An educated man in Western Europe at this time was only just beginning to have some accurate glimmerings of his own white Christian history. How would he view a "heathen savage?"

Benjamin Church liked Indians and was liked by them. That was his secret. From his earliest planting in Little Compton—to the end of his days, they got along. He studied them, admired them, jollied them, dealt fairly with them. He saw in them splendid fighters. They saw in him a splendid captain. They liked to be on the winning side and they took the field with him again and again.

He must have felt protective about them, but when he and Annawon spent an hour together in the dead of that final night, measuring each other in silence, there was no inequality between them.

He knew all about the Indian's "savagery" and he would use his knowledge as a weapon of war in the later expeditions to threaten the French with Indian atrocities if they refused to restrain their own Indians. But he is untouched by the hatred and hysteria which fills the conventional history. He took it for granted that the Indian, if he valued his own survival, should recognize English authority and on that basis he was all for live and let live. No one was less committed to a war of extermination than Benjamin Church.

The decay of the loyal Indian in New England, his eventual disappearance from Sakonnet Point and from every other nook and cranny in the land of his fathers, was beyond Church's vision. He would have felt saddened without them.

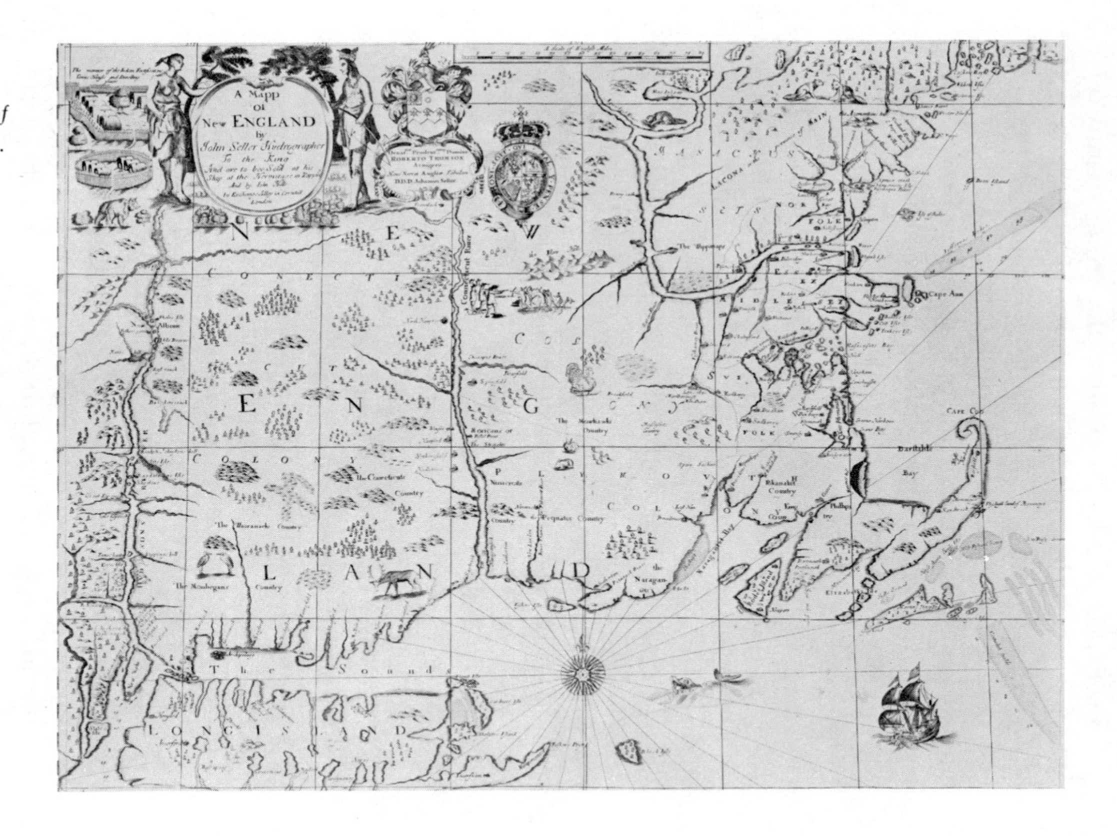

John Seller's Map of New England, 1675.

To The Reader

The subject of this following narrative offering itself to your friendly perusal relates to the former and later wars of New England, which I myself was not a little concerned in. For in the year 1675 that unhappy and bloody Indian War broke out in Plymouth Colony where I was then building and beginning a plantation at a place called by the Indians, Sekonit, and since by the English, Little Compton. I was the first Englishman that built upon that neck, which was full of Indians. My head and hands were full about settling a new plantation where nothing was brought to, no preparation of dwelling house, or out-housing or fencing made. Horses and cattle were to be provided, ground to be cleared and broken up, and the uttermost caution to be used to keep myself free from offending my Indian neighbors all round about me.

While I was thus busily employed and all my time and strength laid out in this laborious undertaking, I received a commission from the Government to engage in their defence. And with my commission I received another heart inclining me to put forth my strength in military service. And through the grace of God I was spirited for that work, and direction in it was renewed to me day by day. And although many of the actions that I was concerned in were very difficult and dangerous, yet myself and those that went with me voluntarily in the service had our lives for the most part wonderfully preserved by the overruling hand of the Almighty, from first to last, which doth aloud bespeak our praises; and to declare His wonderful works is our indispensable duty. I was ever very sensible of my own littleness and unfitness to be employed in such great services, but calling to mind that God is strong, I endeavored to put all my confidence in Him, and by His almighty power was carried through every difficult action; and my desire is that His name may have the praise.

It was ever my intent, having laid myself under a solemn promise, that the many and repeated favors of God to myself and those with me in the service might be published for generations to come. And now my great age requiring my dismission from service in the militia, and to put off my armor, I am willing that the great and glorious works of Almighty God to us children of men should appear to the world. And, having my minutes by me, my son has taken the care and pains to collect from them the ensuing narrative of many passages relating to the former and later wars, which I have had the perusal of, and find nothing amiss as to the truth of it, and with as little reflection upon any particular person as might be, either alive or dead.

And seeing every particle of historical truth is precious, I hope the reader will pass a favorable censure upon an old soldier telling of the many ran-counters he has had and yet is come off alive. It is a pleasure to remember what a great number of families in this and the neighboring provinces in New England did during the war enjoy a great measure of liberty and peace by the hazardous stations and marches of those engaged in military exercises, who were a wall unto them on this side and on that side. I desire prayers that I may be enabled well to accomplish my spiritual warfare, and that I may be more than conqueror through Jesus Christ loving of me.

Benjamin Church

Entertaining Passages Relating to Philip's War which began in the Year 1675 With the Proceedings of Benjamin Church Esquire

In the year 1674 Mr. Benjamin Church of Duxbury, being providentially at Plymouth in the time of the Court, fell into acquaintance with Captain John Almy, of Rhode Island. Captain Almy with great importunity, invited him to ride with him and view that part of Plymouth Colony that lay next to Rhode Island known then by their Indian names of Pocasset[1] and Sogkonate.[2] Among other arguments to persuade him, he told him the soil was very rich and the situation pleasant. Persuades him by all means to purchase of the Company some of the Court grant rights. He accepted his invitation, views the country, and was pleased with it; makes a purchase, settled a farm, found the gentlemen of the Island very civil and obliging. And being himself a person of uncommon activity and industry, he soon erected two buildings upon his farm and gained a good acquaintance with the natives, got much into their favor, and was in a little time in great esteem among them.

The next spring advancing, while Mr. Church was diligently settling his new farm, stocking, leasing, and dispos-

Entertaining Passages

Relating to

Philip's WAR which began in the Year, 1675.

With the Proceedings of

Benj. Church Esqr;

IN the Year 1674. Mr. *Benjamin Church* of *Duxbury* being providentially at *Plymouth* in the time of the Court, fell into acquaintance with Capt. *John Almy* of *Rhode-Island*. Capt. *Almy* with great importunity invited him to ride with him, and view that part of *Plymouth* Colony that lay next to *Rhode-Island*, known then by their Indian Names of *Pocasset* & *Segkonate*. Among other arguments to perswade him, he told him, the Soil was very rich, and the Situation pleasant. Perswades him by all means, to purchase of the Company some of the Court grant rights. He accepted his invitation, views the Country, & was pleased with it; makes a purchase, settled a Farm, found the Gentlemen of the Island very Civil & obliging. And being himself a Person of uncommon Activity and Industry, he soon erected two buildings upon his Farm, and gain'd a good acquaintance with the Natives: got much into their favour, and was in a little time in great esteem among them.

The next Spring advancing, while Mr. *Church* was diligently Settling his new Farm, stocking, leasing & disposing of his Affairs, and had a fine prospect of doing no small things; and hoping that his good succes would be inviting unto other good Men to become his Neighbours; Behold! the rumour of a War between the *English* and the Natives gave check to his projects. People began to be very jealous of the *Indians*, and indeed they had no small reason to suspect that they had form'd a design of War upon the *English*. Mr. *Church* had it daily suggested to him that the Indians were plotting a bloody design. That *Philip* the great *Mount-hope* Sachem was Leader therein: and so it prov'd, he was sending his Messengers to all the

First Page of the First Edition, 1716.

ing of his affairs and had a fine prospect of doing no small things; and hoping that his good success would be inviting unto other good men to become his neighbors, behold! the rumor of a war between the English and the natives gave check to his projects. People began to be very jealous of the Indians, and indeed they had no small reason to suspect that they had formed a design of war upon the English. Mr. Church had it daily suggested to him that the Indians were plotting a bloody design, that Philip, the great Mount-hope sachem was leader therein; and so it proved: he was sending his messengers to all the neighboring sachems to engage them in confederacy with him in the war.

With Awashonks, Queen of the Sakonnets

Among the rest he sent six men to Awashonks, squaw-sachem of the Sogkonate Indians, to engage her in his interests. Awashonks so far listened unto them as to call her subjects together to make a great dance, which is the custom of that nation when they advise about momentous affairs. But what does Awashonks do but sends away two of her men that well understood the English language (Sassamon and George by name) to invite Mr. Church to the dance. Mr. Church, upon the invitation, immediately takes with him Charles Hazelton, his tenant's son, who well understood the Indian language, and rid down to the place appointed where they found hundreds of Indians gathered together from all parts of her dominion. Awashonks herself in a foaming sweat was leading the dance. But she was no sooner sensible of Mr. Church's arrival but she broke off, sat down, calls her nobles round her, orders Mr. Church to be invited into her presence. Complements being passed, and each one taking seats, she told him King Philip had sent six men of his with two of her people that had been over at Mount-hope, to draw her into a confederacy with him in a war with the English. Desiring him to give her his advice in the case, and to tell her the truth whether the Umpame[1] men (as Philip had told her) were gathering a great army to invade Philip's country. He assured her he would tell her the truth and give her his best advice. Then he told her it was but a few days since he came from Plymouth, and the English were then making no preparations for war; that he was in company with the principal gentlemen of the Government, who had no discourse at all about war, and he believed no thoughts about it. He asked her whether she thought he would have brought up his goods to settle in that place if he apprehended an entering into war with so near a neighbor. She seemed to be somewhat convinced by his talk, and said she believed he spoke the truth.

Then she called for the Mount-hope men, who made a formidable appearance with their faces painted and their hair trimmed up in comb-fashion, with their powder horns and shot bags at their backs, which, among that nation, is the posture and figure of preparedness for war. She told Mr. Church, these were the persons that had brought her the report of the English preparation for war. And then told them what Mr. Church had said in answer to it.

Upon this began a warm talk among the Indians, but 'twas soon quashed, and Awashonks proceeded to tell Mr. Church that Philip's message to her was that unless she would forthwith enter into a confederacy with him in a war against the English, he would send his men over privately to kill the English cattle and burn their houses on that side the river, which would provoke the English to fall upon her, whom they would without doubt sup-

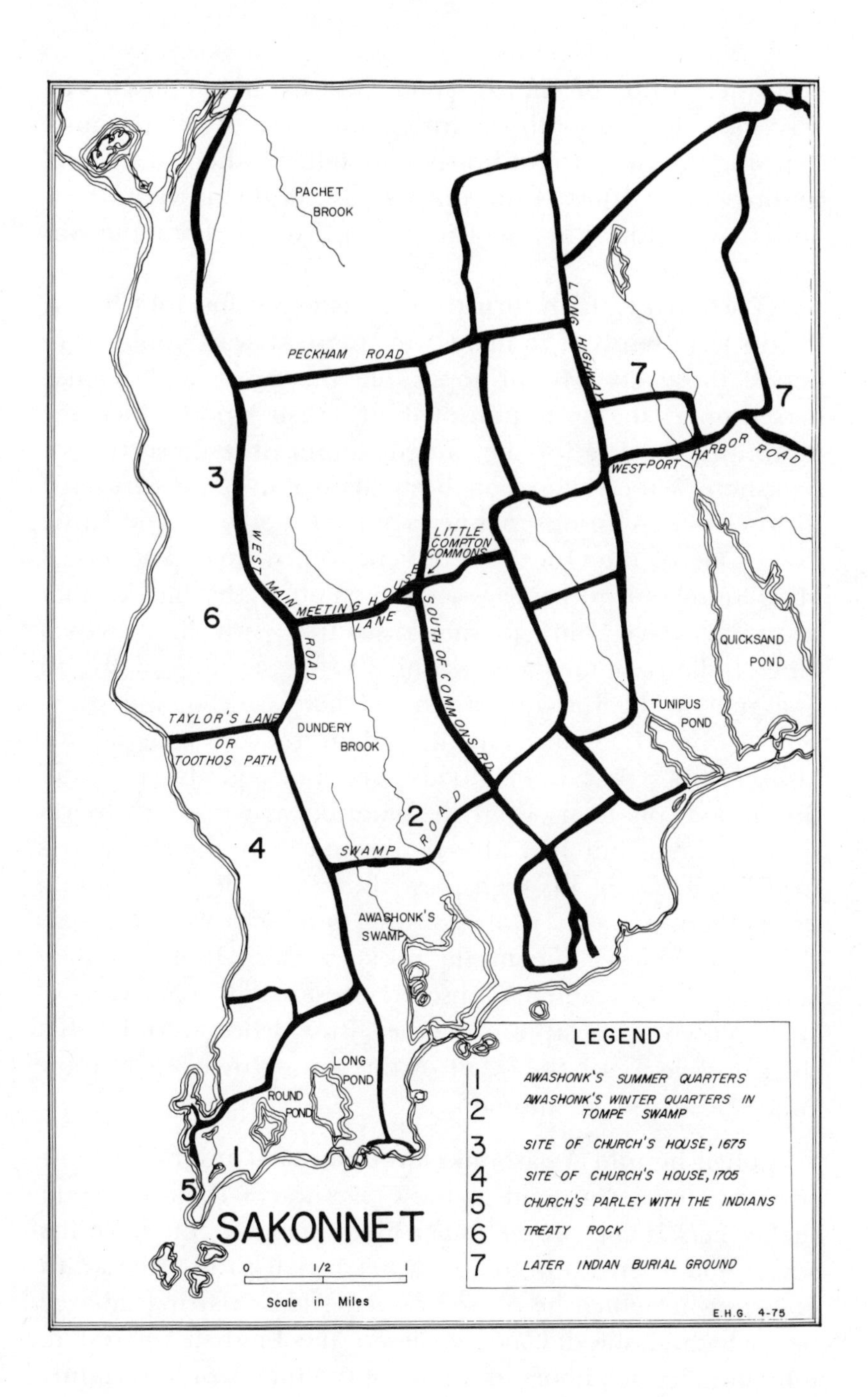
PACHET
BROOK
PECKHAM ROAD
LONG HIGHWAY
7
7
WESTPORT HARBOR ROAD
3
LITTLE
COMPTON
COMMONS
WEST MAIN ROAD
MEETING HOUSE LANE
SOUTH OF COMMONS RD.
6
QUICKSAND
POND
TUNIPUS
POND
TAYLOR'S LANE
OR
TOOTHOS PATH
DUNDERY
BROOK
2
SWAMP ROAD
4
AWASHONK'S
SWAMP
LONG
POND
ROUND
POND
1
5
SAKONNET
0 1/2 1
Scale in Miles
LEGEND
1 AWASHONK'S SUMMER QUARTERS
2 AWASHONK'S WINTER QUARTERS IN TOMPE SWAMP
3 SITE OF CHURCH'S HOUSE, 1675
4 SITE OF CHURCH'S HOUSE, 1705
5 CHURCH'S PARLEY WITH THE INDIANS
6 TREATY ROCK
7 LATER INDIAN BURIAL GROUND
E.H.G. 4-75

pose the author of the mischief. Mr. Church told her he was sorry to see so threatening an aspect of affairs, and, stepping to the Mount-hopes, he felt of their bags and finding them filled with bullets, asked them what those bullets were for. They scoffingly replied, to shoot pigeons with.

Then Mr. Church turned to Awashonks and told her, if Philip were resolved to make war, her best way would be to knock those six Mount-hopes on the head and shelter herself under the protection of the English, upon which the Mount-hopes were for the present dumb. But those two of Awashonk's men who had been at Mount-hope expressed themselves in a furious manner against his advice. And Little Eyes[2], one of the Queen's Council, joined them and urged Mr. Church to go aside with him among the bushes that he might have some private discourse with him, which other Indians immediately forbid, being sensible of his ill design; but the Indians began to [take] side[s] and grow very warm. Mr. Church with undaunted courage told the Mount-hopes they were bloody wretches and thirsted after the blood of their English neighbors, who had never injured them, but had always abounded in their kindness to them. That for his own part, though he desired nothing more than peace, yet, if nothing but war would satisfy them, he believed he should prove a sharp thorn in their sides; bid the company observe those men that were of such bloody disposition, whether Providence would suffer them to live to see the event of the war, which others more peaceably disposed might do.

Then he told Awashonks he thought it might be most advisable for her to send to the Governor of Plymouth and shelter herself and people under his protection. She liked his advice and desired him to go on her behalf to the Plymouth government, which he consented to. And at parting advised her, whatever she did, not to desert the English interest to join with her neighbors in a rebellion which would certainly prove fatal to her. (He moved none of his goods from his house that there might not be the least umbrage from such an action.) She thanked him for his advice and sent two of her men to guard him to his house, which, when they came there, urged him to take care to secure his goods, which he refused for the reasons before-mentioned. But desired the Indians that if what they feared should happen, they would take care of what he left and directed them to a place in the woods where they should dispose them; which they faithfully observed.

With Weetamoo, Queen of the Pocassets

He took his leave of his guard, and bid them tell their mistress, if she continued steady in her dependence on the English and kept within her own limits of Sogkonate, he would see her again quickly, and then hastened away to Pocasset, where he met with Peter Nunnuit, the husband of the Queen of Pocasset, who was just then come over in a canoe from Mount-hope. Peter told him that there would certainly be war, for Philip had held a dance of several weeks' continuance and had entertained the young men from all parts of the country. And added that Philip expected to be sent for to Plymouth to be examined about Sassamon's death, who was murdered at Assawomset-Ponds, knowing himself guilty of contriving that murder. The same Peter told him that he saw Mr. James Brown of Swanzey and Mr. Samuel Gorton who was an interpreter and two other men who brought a letter from the Governor of Plymouth to Philip. He observed to him further that the young men were very eager to begin the war and would fain have killed Mr. Brown, but Philip prevented it, telling them that his father had charged him to show kindness to Mr. Brown. In short, Philip was forced to promise them that on the next Lord's Day when the English were gone to meeting they should rifle their houses, and from that time forward kill their cattle.

Peter desired Mr. Church to go and see his wife, who was but up the hill.[1] He went and found but few of her people with her. She said they were all gone, against her will, to the dances, and she much feared there would be a war. Mr. Church advised her to go to the Island and secure herself and those that were with her, and send to the Governor of Plymouth, who she knew was her friend, and so left her, resolving to hasten to Plymouth and wait on the Governor. And he was so expeditious that he was with the Governor early next morning,[2] though he waited on some of the magistrates by the way, who were of the Council of War, and also met him at the Governor's. He gave them an account of his observations and discoveries, which confirmed their former intelligences and hastened their preparation for defence.

Philip, according to his promise to his people, permitted them to march out of the Neck[3] on the next Lord's Day,[4] when they plundered the nearest houses that the inhabitants had deserted, but as yet offered no violence to the people, at least none were killed. However, the alarm was given by their numbers and hostile equipage and by the prey they made of what they could find in the forsaken houses.

The Mount Hope Campaign

An express came the same day to the Governor, who immediately gave order to the captains of the towns to march the greatest part of their companies and to rendezvous at Taunton on Monday night, where Major Bradford[1] was to receive them and dispose them under Captain (now made Major) Cutworth[2] of Situate [Scituate.] The Governor desired Mr. Church to give them his company and to use his interest in their behalf with the gentlemen of Rhode Island. He complied with it, and they marched the next day.[3] Major Bradford desired Mr. Church with a commanded party consisting of English and some friend-Indians, to march in the front at some distance from the main body. Their orders were to keep so far before as not be in sight of the army. And so they did, for by the way they killed a deer, flayed, roasted, and ate the most of him before the army came up with them. But the Plymouth forces soon arrived at Swanzey, and were posted at Major Brown's and Mr. Miles's garrisons[4] chiefly, and were there soon joined with those that came from Massachusetts,[5] who had entered into a confederacy with their Plymouth brethen against the perfidious heathen.

The enemy, who began their hostilities with plundering and destroying cattle, did not long content themselves with that game. They thirsted for English blood and they soon broached it, killing two men in the way not far from Mr. Miles's garrison. And soon after, eight more at Mattapoiset,[6] upon whose bodies they exercised more than brutish bar-

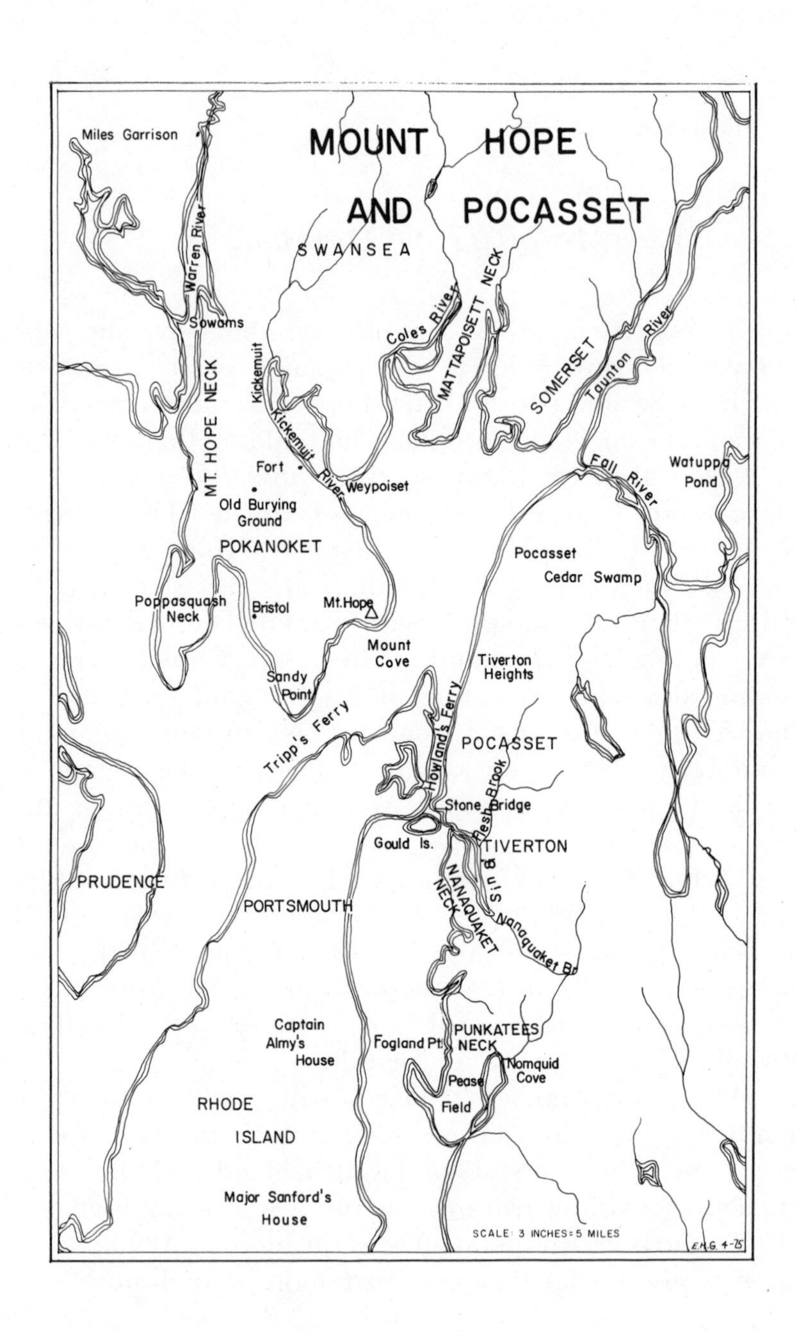
MOUNT HOPE
AND POCASSET
Miles Garrison
Warren River
SWANSEA
Sowams
Coles River
MATTAPOISETT NECK
SOMERSET
Taunton River
Kickemuit
Kickemuit River
MT. HOPE NECK
Fort
Weypoiset
Old Burying Ground
POKANOKET
Fall River
Watuppa Pond
Pocasset
Cedar Swamp
Poppasquash Neck
Bristol
Mt. Hope
Mount Cove
Tiverton Heights
Sandy Point
Tripp's Ferry
Howland's Ferry
POCASSET
Fresh Brook
Stone Bridge
Gould Is.
TIVERTON
Sin Brook
PRUDENCE
PORTSMOUTH
NANAQUAKET NECK
Nanaquaket Br
Captain Almy's House
Fogland Pt.
PUNKATEES NECK
Nomquid Cove
Pease Field
RHODE ISLAND
Major Sanford's House
SCALE: 3 INCHES=5 MILES
E.H.G. 4-75

barities, beheading, dismembering, and mangling them and exposing them in the most inhumane manner, which gashed and ghostly objects struck a damp on all beholders.

The enemy, flushed with these exploits, grew yet bolder and skulking everywhere in the bushes, shot at all passengers and killed many that ventured abroad. They came so near as to shoot down two sentinels at Mr. Miles's garrison, under the very noses of most of our forces. These provocations drew out the resentments of some of Captain Prentice's troop, who desired they might have liberty to go out and seek the enemy in their own quarters. Quartermasters Gill and Belcher commanded the parties drawn out, who earnestly desired Mr. Church's company. They provided him a horse and furniture (his own being out of the way); he readily complied with their desires and was soon mounted.

This party were no sooner over Miles's bridge but were fired on by an ambuscado of about a dozen Indians, as they were afterwards discovered to be. When they drew off, the pilot was mortally wounded; Mr. Belcher received a shot in his knee, and his horse was killed under him; Mr. Gill was struck with a musket ball on the side of his belly, but being clad with a buff coat and some thickness of paper under it, it never broke his skin. The troopers were surprised to see both their commanders wounded, and wheeled off. But Mr. Church persuaded, at length stormed and stamped, and told them it was a shame to run and leave a wounded man there to become a prey to the barbarous enemy. For the pilot yet sat his horse, though so mazed with the shot as not to have sense to guide him. Mr. Gill seconded him and offered, though much disenabled, to assist in bringing him off. Mr. Church asked a stranger who gave them his company in that action, if he would go with him and fetch off the wounded man. He readily consented. They with Mr. Gill went, but the wounded man fainted and fell off his horse before they came to him; but Mr. Church and the stranger dismounted, took up the man, dead, and laid him before Mr. Gill on his horse. Mr.

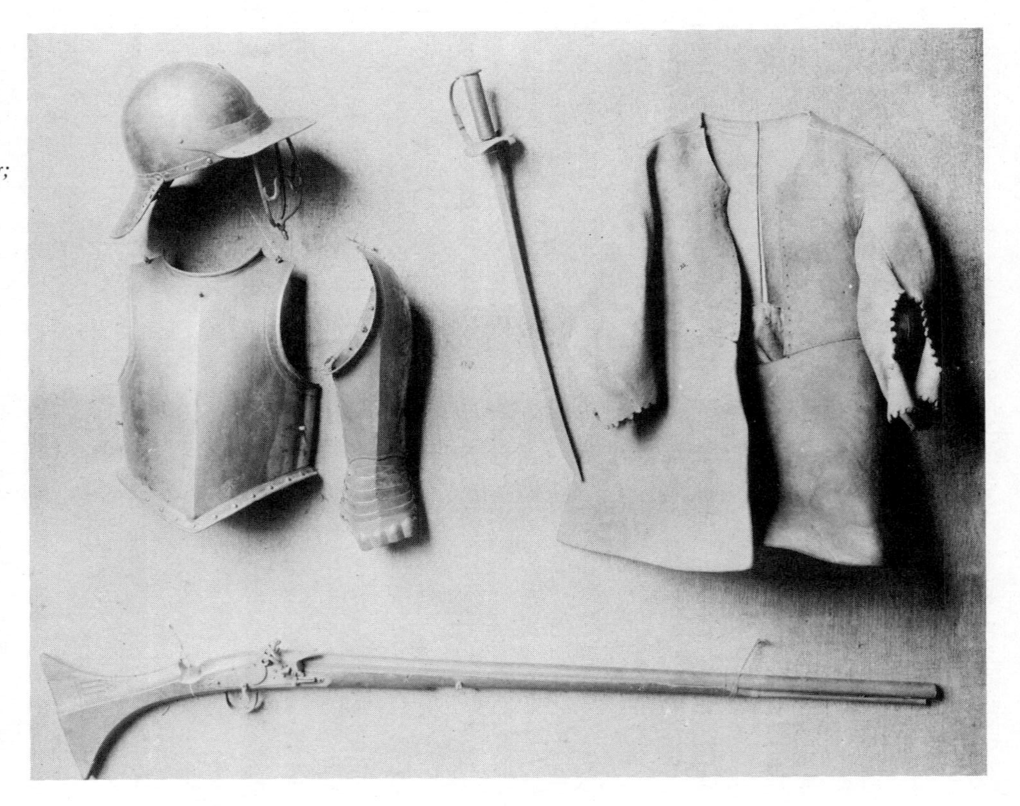

Church's Sword; Leverett's Jerkin; Fitz John Winthrop's Armor; Andrus' Gun.

Church told the other two, if they would take care of the dead man, he would go and fetch his horse back, which was going off the cassey [i.e., causeway] toward the enemy. But before he got over the cassey, he saw the enemy run to the right into the neck. He brought back the horse and called earnestly and repeatedly to the army to come over and fight the enemy. And, while he stood calling and persuading, the skulking enemy returned to their old stand, and all discharged their guns at him at one clap; though every shot missed him, yet one of the army on the other side of the river received one of the balls in his foot. Mr. Church now began (no succor coming to him) to think it time to retreat, saying, "The Lord have mercy on us if such a handful of Indians shall thus dare such an army!"

Upon this it was immediately resolved,[7] and orders were given to march down into the neck, and having passed the bridge and cassey, the direction was to extend both wings, which being not well headed by those that remained in the center, some of them mistook their friends for their enemies and made fire upon them on the right wing and wounded that noble, heroic youth, Ensign Savage, in the thigh, but it happily proved but a flesh wound. They marched[8] until they came to the narrow of the neck, at a place called Keekkamuit, where they took down the heads of eight Englishmen that were killed at the head of Metapoiset Neck and set upon poles, after the barbarous manner of those savages. There Philip had staved all his drums and conveyed all his canoes to the east side of Metapoist River. Hence it was concluded by those that were acquainted with the motions of those people that they had quitted the neck. Mr. Church told'em that Philip was doubtless gone over to Pocasset side to engage those Indians in rebellion with him, which they soon found to be true. The enemy were not really beaten out of Mount-hope Neck, though 'twas true they fled from thence; yet it was before any pursued them. It was but to strengthen themselves and to gain a more advantageous post. However some, and not a few, pleased themselves with the fancy of a mighty conquest.

A grand council was held, and a resolve passed to build a fort there to maintain the first ground they had gained by the Indians leaving it to them. And, to speak the truth, it must be said that as they gained not that field by their sword nor their bow, so it was rather their fear than their courage that obliged them to set up the marks of their conquest. Mr. Church looked upon it,and talk of it,with contempt and urged hard the pursuing the enemy on Pocasset side, and with the greater earnestness because of his promise made to Awashonks, before mentioned. The council adjourned themselves from Mount-hope to Rehoboth, where Mr. Treasurer Southworth[9] being weary of his charge of Commissary General (provision being scarce and difficult to be obtained for the army, that now lay still to cover the people from nobody, while they were building a fort for nothing), retired; and the power and trouble of that post was left with Mr. Church, who still urged the commanding officers to move over to Pocasset side to pursue the enemy and kill Philip, which would, in his opinion, be more probable to keep possession of the neck than to tarry to build a fort. He was still restless on that side of the river, and the rather because of his promise to the squaw sachem of Sogkonate. And Captain Fuller also urged the same, until at length there came further order concerning the fort. And withal, an order for Captain Fuller with six files to cross the river to the side so much insisted on, and to try if he could get speech with any of the Pocasset or Sogkonate Indians, and that Mr. Church should go his second.

Upon the Captain's receiving his orders, he asked Mr. Church whether he was willing to engage in this enterprise. To whom 'twas indeed too agreeable to be declined, though he thought the enterprise was hazardous enough for them to have more men assigned them. Captain Fuller told him that for his own part he was grown ancient and heavy; he feared the travel and fatigue would be too much for him. But Mr. Church urged him and told him he would cheerfully excuse him his hardship and travel and take that part to himself, if he might but go, for he had rather do anything in the world than stay there to build the fort.

The Pocasset Campaign

Then they drew out the number assigned them and marched the same night to the ferry and were transported to Rhode Island, from whence the next night they got a passage over to Pocasset side in Rhode-Island boats and concluded there to dispose themselves in two ambuscados before day, hoping to surprise some of the enemy by their falling into one or other of their ambushments. But Captain Fuller's party being troubled with the epidemical plague of lust after tobacco, must needs strike fire to smoke it, and thereby discovered themselves to a party of the enemy coming up to them, who immediately fled with great precipitation.

This ambuscado drew off about break of day, perceiving they were discovered, the other continued in their post until the time assigned them, and the light and heat of the sun rendered their station both insignificant and troublesome, and then returned unto the place of rendezvous, where they were acquainted with the other party's disappointment and the occasion of it. Mr. Church calls for the breakfast he had ordered to be brought over in the boat, but the man that had the charge of it confessed that he was asleep when the boatsmen called him and in haste came away and never thought of it. It happened that Mr. Church had a few cakes of rusk in his pocket that Madam Cranston (the Governor of

Rhode Island's lady), gave him when he came off the Island, which he divided among the company, which was all the provisions they had.

Mr. Church, after their slender breakfast, proposed to Captain Fuller that he would march in quest of the enemy, with such of the company as would be willing to march with him; which he complied with, though with a great deal of scruple because of his small number and the extreme hazard he foresaw must attend them.

But some of the company had reflected upon Mr. Church that, notwithstanding his talk on the other side of the river, he had not shown them any Indians since they came over. Which now moved him to tell them that if it was their desire to see Indians, he believed he should now soon show them what they should say was enough.

The number allowed him soon drew off to him, which could not be many, because their whole company consisted of no more than thirty-six. They moved toward Sogkonate, until they came to the brook that runs into Nunnaquohqut Neck, where they discovered a fresh and plain track, which they concluded to be from the great pine swamp, about a mile from the road that leads to Sogkonet. "Now," says Mr. Church to his men, "if we follow this track, no doubt but we shall soon see Indians enough." They expressed their willingness to follow the track and moved in it, but had not gone far before one of them narrowly escaped being bit with a rattlesnake. And the woods that the track led them through was haunted much with those snakes which the little company seemed more to be afraid of than the black serpents they were in quest of, and therefore bent their course another way to a place where they thought it probable to find some of the enemy. Had they kept the track to the pine swamp they had been certain of meeting Indians enough, but not so certain that any of them should have returned to give account how many.

The Pease Field Fight

Now they passed down into Punkatees Neck,[1] and in their march discovered a large wigwam full of Indian truck, which the soldiers were for loading themselves with until Mr. Church forbid it, telling them they might expect soon to have their hands full, and business without caring for plunder. Then, crossing the head of the creek into the neck, they again discovered fresh Indian tracks, very lately passed before them into the neck. They then got privately and undiscovered unto the fence of Captain Almy's pease field and divided into two parties. Mr. Church, keeping the one party with himself, sent the other with Lake, that was acquainted with the ground, on the other side. Two Indians were soon discovered coming out of the pease field towards them. When Mr. Church and those that were with him concealed themselves from them by falling flat on the ground; but the other division, not using the same caution, were seen by the enemy, which occasioned them to run; which, when Mr. Church perceived, he showed himself to them and called, telling them he desired but to speak with them and would not hurt them. But they ran, and Church pursued. The Indians climbed over a fence, and one of them, facing about, discharged his piece, but without effect on the English. One of the English soldiers ran up to the fence and fired upon him that had discharged his piece, and they concluded by the yelling they heard that the Indian was wounded; but the Indians soon got into the thickets, whence they saw them no more for the present.

Mr. Church, then marching over a plain piece of ground where the woods were very thick on one side, ordered his little company to march at double distance, to make as big a show (if they should be discovered) as might be. But, before they saw anybody, they were saluted with a volley of fifty or sixty guns. Some bullets came very surprisingly near Mr. Church, who, starting, looked behind him, to see what was become of his men, expecting to have seen half of them dead, but, seeing them all upon their legs and briskly firing at the smokes of the enemy's guns (for that was all that was then to be seen), he blessed God and called to his men not to discharge all their guns at once, lest the enemy should take the advantage of such an opportunity to run upon them with their hatchets.

Their next motion was immediately into the pease field. When they came to the fence, Mr. Church bid as many as had not discharged their guns to clap under the fence and lie close, while the other, at some distance in the field, stood to charge, hoping that if the enemy should creep to the fence to gain a shot at those that were charging their guns, they might be surprised by those that lay under the fence. But casting his eyes to the side of the hill above them, the hill seemed to move, being covered over with Indians, with their bright guns glittering in the sun and running in a circumference with a design to surround them.

Seeing such multitudes surrounding him and his little company, it put him upon thinking what was become of the boats that were ordered to attend him. And, looking up, he spied them ashore at Sandy Point, on the Island side of the river, with a number of horse and foot by them, and wondered what should be the occasion, until he was afterwards informed that the boats had been over that morning from the Island and had landed a party of men at Fogland, that were designed in Punkatees Neck to fetch off some cattle and horses, but were ambuscadoed and many of them wounded by the enemy.

Now our gentleman's courage and conduct were both put to the test; he encourages his men and orders some to run and take a wall to shelter before the enemy gained it. 'Twas time for them now to think of escaping if they knew which way. Mr. Church orders his men to strip to their white shirts, that the Islanders might discover them to be Englishmen, and then orders three guns to be fired distinct, hoping it might be observed by their friends on the opposite shore. The men that were ordered to take the wall, being very hungry, stopped a while among the pease to gather a few, being about four rod from the wall. The enemy, from behind it, hailed them with a shower of bullets, but soon all but one came tumbling over an old hedge down the bank where Mr. Church and the rest were, and told him that his brother, B. Southworth,[2] who was the man that was missing, was killed, that they saw him fall. And so they did indeed see him fall, but 'twas without a shot, and lay no longer than till he had opportunity to clap a bullet into one of the enemy's forehead, and then came running to his company.

The meanness of the English's powder was now their greatest misfortune when they were immediately upon this beset with multitudes of Indians, who possessed themselves of every rock, stump, tree, or fence that was in sight, firing upon them without ceasing, while they had no other shelter but a small bank and a bit of a water fence. And yet, to add to the disadvantage of this little handful of distressed men, the Indians also possessed themselves of the ruins of a stone house that overlooked them, and of the black rocks to the southward of them,[3] so that now they had no way to prevent lying quite open to some or other of the enemy but to heap up stones before them, as they did, and still bravely and wonderfully defended themselves against all the numbers of the enemy.

At length came over one of the boats from the Island shore, but the enemy plied their shot so warmly to her as made her keep at some distance. Mr. Church desired them to

Sloop, about 1680. *(Right) Statue of Massasoit, Plymouth.*

send their canoe ashore to fetch them on board, but no persuasions nor arguments could prevail with them to bring their canoe to shore. Which some of Mr. Church's men perceiving, began to cry out, For God's sake to take them off, for their ammunition was spent. Mr. Church, being sensible of the danger of the enemy's hearing their complaints and being made acquainted with the weakness and scantiness of their ammunition, fiercely called to the boat's master and bid [him] either send his canoe ashore or else begone presently or he would fire upon him.

Away goes the boat and leaves them still to shift for themselves. But then another difficulty arose; the enemy, seeing the boat leave them, were reanimated and fired thicker and faster than ever. Upon which, some of the men that were lightest of foot began to talk of attempting an escape by flight, until Mr. Church solidly convinced them of the impracticableness of it, and encouraged them yet; told them that he had observed so much of the remarkable and wonderful Providence of God hitherto preserving them, that encouraged him to believe with much confidence that God would yet preserve them; that not a hair of their head should fall to the ground, bid them be patient, courageous, and prudently sparing of their ammunition, and he made no doubt but they should come well off yet, etc., until his little army again resolve, one and all, to stay with and stick by him. One of them, by Mr. Church's order, was pitching a flat stone up on end before him in the sand when a bullet from the enemy, with a full force, struck the stone while he was pitching it on end, which put the poor fellow to a miserable start, till Mr. Church called upon him to observe how God directed the bullets that the enemy could not hit him when in the same place, yet could hit the stone as it was erected.

While they were thus making the best defence they could against their numerous enemies that made the woods ring with their constant yelling and shouting; and, night coming on, somebody told Mr. Church they spied a sloop up the river as far as Gold [Gould] Island that seemed to be coming down towards them. He looked up and told them succor was now coming, for he believed it was Captain Golding[4] whom he knew to be a man for business and would certainly fetch them off if he came. The wind being fair, the vessel was soon with them; and Captain Golding it was. Mr. Church (as soon as they came to speak one with another) desired him to come to anchor at such a distance from the shore that he might veer out his cable and ride afloat, and let slip his canoe that it might drive ashore, which directions Captain Golding observed; but the enemy gave him such a warm salute that his sails, color, and stern were full of bullet holes.

The canoe came ashore but was so small that she would not bear above two men at a time, and when two were got aboard, they turned her loose to drive ashore for two more, and the sloop's company kept the Indians in play the while. But when at last it came to Mr. Church's turn to go aboard, he had left his hat and cutlass at the well where he went to drink when he first came down. He told his company he would never go off and leave his hat and cutlass for the Indians; they should never have that to reflect upon him. Though he was much dissuaded from it, yet he would go fetch them. He put all the powder he had left into his gun (and a poor charge it was) and went presenting his gun at the enemy until he took up what he went for. At his return he discharged his gun at the enemy to bid them farewell, for that time; but had not powder enough to carry the bullet halfway to them.

Two bullets from the enemy struck the canoe as he went on board; one grazed the hair of his head a little before; another struck in a small stake that stood right against the middle of his breast.

Now this gentleman with his army, making in all 20 men, himself and his pilot being numbered with them, got all safe aboard after six hours' engagement with 300 Indians, whose number we were told afterwards by some of themselves. A deliverance which that good gentleman often mentions to the glory of God and His protecting providence.

The next day,[5] meeting with the rest of their little company, whom he had left at Pocasset (that had also a small skirmish with the Indians, and had two men wounded), they returned to the Mount-hope garrison, which Mr. Church used to call the loosing fort. Mr. Church, then returning to the Island to seek provisions for the army meets with Alderman,[6] a noted Indian that was just come over from the squaw sachem's Cape of Pocasset, having deserted from her, and had brought over his family, who gave him an account of the state of the Indians and where each of the sagamores' headquarters were. Mr. Church then discoursed with some who knew the spot well where the Indians said Weetamore's headquarters were, and offered their services to pilot him. With this news he hastened to the Mount-hope garrison. The army expressed their readiness to embrace such an opportunity.

Hunting Weetamoo and Philip

All the ablest soldiers were now immediately drawn off, equipped, and dispatched upon this design, under the command of a certain officer. And, having marched about two miles, viz., until they came to the cove that lies S.W. from the Mount, where orders were given for an halt.[1] The commander-in-chief told them he thought it proper to take advice before he went any further, called Mr. Church and the pilot and asked them how they knew that Philip and all his men were not by that time got to Weetamore's camp, or that all her own men were not by that time returned to her again? With many more frightful questions.

Mr. Church told him they had acquainted him with as much as they knew, and that for his part he could discover nothing that need to discourage them from proceeding, that he thought it so practicable that he with the pilot would willingly lead the way to the spot and hazard the brunt. But the chief commander insisted on this: that the enemy's number were so great, and he did not know what numbers more might be added unto them by that time, and his company so small, that he could not think it practicable to attack them. Added, moreover, that if he was sure of killing all the enemy, and knew that he must lose the life of one of his men in the action, he would not attempt it. "Pray, Sir, then," replied Mr. Church, "please to lead your company to yonder windmill on Rhode Island, and there they will be out of danger of being killed by the enemy, and we shall have less trouble to supply them with provisions."

But return he would, and did, unto the garrison, until more strength came to them, and a sloop to transport them to the Fall River, in order to visit Weetamore's camp. Mr. Church, one Baxter and Captain Hunter,[2] an Indian, proffered to go out on the discovery on the left wing, which was accepted. They had not marched above a quarter of a mile before they started three of the enemy. Captain Hunter wounded one of them in his knee, whom, when he came up, he discovered to be his near kinsman; the captive desired favor for his squaw, if she should fall into their hands, but asked none for himself, excepting the liberty of taking a whiff of tobacco, and, while he was taking his whiff, his kinsman with one blow of his hatchet dispatched him.

Proceeding to Weetamore's camp, they were discovered by one of the enemy, who ran in and gave information; upon which a lusty young fellow left his meat upon his spit, running hastily out, told his companions he would kill an Englishman before he ate his dinner; but failed of his design, being no sooner out but shot down. The enemy's fires and what shelter they had was by the edge of a thick cedar swamp, into which on this alarm they betook themselves; and the English as nimbly pursued, but were soon commanded back by their chieftain after they were come within hearing of the cries of their women and children; and so ended that exploit. But, returning to their sloop, the enemy pursued them and wounded two of their men. The next day returned to the Mount-hope garrison.

Soon after this, was Philip's headquarters visited by

some other English forces, but Philip and his gang had the very fortune to escape that Weetamore and hers (but now mentioned) had; they took into a swamp, and their pursuers were commanded back.[3] After this, Dartmouth's distresses required succor; great part of the town being laid desolate and many of the inhabitants killed, the most of Plymouth forces were ordered thither. And coming to Russell's garrison at Poneganset, they met with a number of the enemy that had surrendered themselves prisoners on terms promised by Captain Eels, of the garrison, and Ralph Earl, that persuaded them (by a friend Indian he had employed) to come in. And, had their promises to the Indians been kept, and the Indians fairly treated, 'tis probable that most, if not all the Indians in those parts, had soon followed the example of those that had now surrendered themselves, which would have been a good step towards finishing the war. But, in spite of all that Captain Eels, Church, or Earl could say, argue, plead, or beg, somebody else that had more power in their hands improved it; and, without any regard to the promises made them on their surrendering themselves, they were carried away to Plymouth, there sold, and transported out of the country, being about eight-score persons—an action so hateful to Mr. Church that he opposed it to the loss of the good will and respect of some that before were his good friends.

But while these things were acting at Dartmouth, Philip made his escape, leaving his country, fled over Taunton River and Rehoboth Plain, and Petuxet River, where Captain Edmunds of Providence made some spoil upon [him]; and had probably done more, but was prevented by the coming up of a superior officer that put him by.

And now another fort was built at Pocasset, that proved as troublesome and chargeable as that at Mount-hope; and the remainder of the summer was improved in providing for the forts and forces there maintained, while our enemies were fled some hundreds of miles into the country, near as far as Albany.

Indians Cooking Fish.

The Great Swamp Fight

And now strong suspicions began to arise of the Narraganset Indians, that they were ill-affected and designed mischief; and so the event soon discovered. The next winter they began their hostilities upon the English. The United Colonies then agreed to send an army to suppress them, Governor Winslow to command the army.[1] He, undertaking the expedition, invited Mr. Church to command a company in the expedition, which he declined. Craving excuse from taking commission, he promised to wait upon him as a reformado[2] through the expedition. Having ridden with the General to Boston, and from thence to Rehoboth, upon the General's request he went thence the nearest way over the ferries with Major Smith to his garrison in the Narraganset country to prepare and provide for the coming of General Winslow; who marched round through the country with his army, proposing by night to surprise Pumham (a certain Narraganset sachem) and his town;[3] but, being aware of the approach of our army, made their escape into the deserts.

But Mr. Church, meeting with fair winds, arrived safe at the Major's garrison in the evening.[4] And soon began to enquire after the enemy's resorts, wigwams or sleeping places; and having gained some intelligence, he proposed to the Eldriges and some other brisk hands that he met with, to attempt the surprising of some of the enemy to make a present of to the General, when he should arrive: which might advantage his design. Being brisk blades, they readily complied with the motion and were soon upon their march. The night was very cold but blessed with the moon. Before the day broke they effected their exploit and by the rising of the sun arrived at the Major's garrison, where they met the General and presented him with eighteen of the enemy they had captured. The General, pleased with the exploit, gave them thanks, particularly to Mr. Church, the mover and chief actor of the business. And sending two of them (likely boys) [as] a present to Boston, smiling on Mr. Church, told him that he made no doubt but his faculty would supply them with Indian boys enough before the war was ended.

Their next move[5] was to a swamp which the Indians had fortified with a fort. Mr. Church rode in the General's guard when the bloody engagement began; but being impatient of being out of the heat of the action, importunately begged leave of the General that he might run down to the assistance of his friends. The General yielded to his request, provided he could rally some hands to go with him. Thirty men immediately drew out and followed him. They entered the swamp and passed over the log that was the passage into the fort,[6] where they saw many men and several valiant captains lie slain. Mr. Church, spying Captain Gardner of Salem amidst the wigwams in the east end of the fort, made towards him, but on a sudden, while they were looking each other in the face, Captain Gardner settled down. Mr. Church stepped to him and, seeing the blood run down his cheek, lifted up his cap, and called him by his name. He looked up in his face, but spoke not a word, being mortally shot through the head. And, observing his wound, Mr. Church found the ball entered his head on the side that was next the upland where the English entered the swamp. Upon which, having ordered some care to be taken of the Captain, he dispatched information to the General that the best and forwardest of his army that hazarded their lives to enter the fort, upon the muzzle of the enemy's guns, were shot in their backs and killed by them that lay behind.

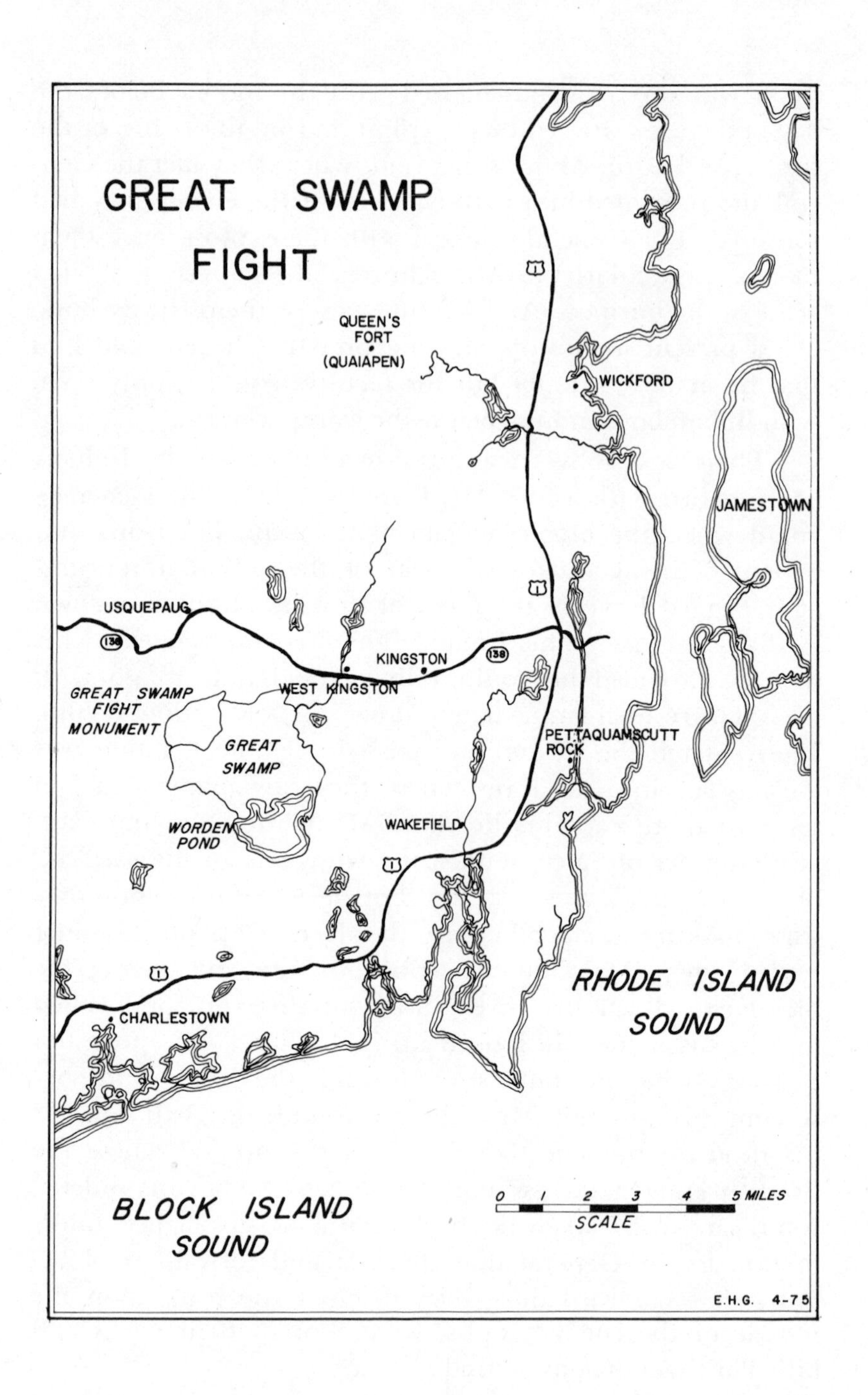
GREAT SWAMP FIGHT
QUEEN'S FORT (QUAIAPEN)
WICKFORD
JAMESTOWN
USQUEPAUG
KINGSTON
WEST KINGSTON
GREAT SWAMP FIGHT MONUMENT
GREAT SWAMP
PETTAQUAMSCUTT ROCK
WORDEN POND
WAKEFIELD
CHARLESTOWN
RHODE ISLAND SOUND
BLOCK ISLAND SOUND
0 1 2 3 4 5 MILES
SCALE
E.H.G. 4-75

Palisaded Indian Village, Pomeiock, North Carolina.

Mr. Church with his small company hastened out of the fort (that the English were now possessed of) to get a shot at the Indians that were in the swamp, and kept firing upon them. He soon met with a broad bloody track, where the enemy had fled with their wounded men. Following hard in the track, he soon spied one of the enemy, who clapped his gun across his breast, made towards Mr. Church, and beckoned to him with his hand. Mr. Church immediately commanded no man to hurt him, hoping by him to have gained some intelligence of the enemy that might be of advantage; but it unhappily fell out that a fellow that had lagged behind coming up, shot down the Indian, to Mr. Church's great grief and disappointment. But immediately they heard a great shout of the enemy, which seemed to be behind them, or between them and the fort; and discovered them running from tree to tree to gain advantages of firing upon the English that were in the fort. Mr. Church's great difficulty now was how to discover himself to his friends in the fort, using several inventions, till at length [he] gained an opportunity to call to and inform a sergeant in the fort that he was there and might be exposed to their shots unless they observed it.

By this time he discovered a number of the enemy almost within shot of him, making towards the fort. Mr. Church and his company were favored by a heap of brush that was between them and the enemy and prevented their being discovered to them. Mr. Church had given his men their particular orders for firing upon the enemy; and as they were rising up to make their shot, the aforementioned sergeant in the fort called out to them, for God's sake not to fire, for he believed they were some of their friend-Indians.[7] They clapped down again but were soon sensible of the sergeant's mistake. The enemy got to the top of the tree, the body whereof the sergeant stood upon, and there clapped down out of sight of the fort, but, all this while, never discovered Mr. Church, who observed them to keep gathering unto that place, until there seemed to be a formidable black heap of them.

"Now, brave boys," said Mr. Church to his men, "if we mind our hits, we may have a brave shot, and let our sign for firing on them be their rising up to fire into the fort." It was not long before the Indians, rising up as one body, designed to pour a volley into the fort, when our Church nimbly started up and gave them such a round volley and unexpected clap on their backs, that they who escaped with their lives were so surprised that they scampered, they knew not whither themselves.

Church Wounded

About a dozen of them ran right over the log into the fort and took into a sort of hovel that was built with poles, after the manner of a corn crib. Mr. Church's men, having their cartridges fixed, were soon ready to obey his order, which was immediately to charge and run upon the hovel and over-set it, calling as he ran on to some that were in the fort to assist him in over-setting of it. They no sooner came to face the enemy's shelter, but Mr. Church discovered that one of them had found a hole to point his gun through, right at him; but, however, encouraged his company and ran right on till he was struck with three bullets, one in his thigh, which was near half of it cut off as it glanced on the joint of the hip bone; another through the gatherings of his breeches and draws, with a small flesh wound; a third pierced his pocket and wounded a pair of mittens that he had borrowed of Captain Prentice, [which] being wrapped up together, had the misfortune of having many holes cut through them with one bullet. But, however, he made shift to keep on his legs and nimbly discharged his gun at them that wounded him.

Being disenabled now to go a step, his men would have carried him off, but he forbid their touching him until they had perfected their project of over-setting the enemy's shelter; bid them run, for now the Indians had no guns charged. While he was urging them to run on, the Indians began to shoot arrows, and with one pierced through the arm of an Englishman that had hold of Mr. Church's arm to support him.

The English, in short, were discouraged and drew back. And by this time the English people in the fort had begun to set fire to the wigwams and houses in the fort, which Mr. Church labored hard to prevent. They told him they had orders from the General to burn them; he begged them to forebear until he had discoursed [with] the General; and hastening to him, he begged [him] to spare the wigwams in the fort from fire, told him the wigwams were musketproof, being all lined with baskets and tubs of grain and other provisions sufficient to supply the whole army until the spring of the year, and every wounded man might have a good warm house to lodge in, which otherwise would necessarily perish with the storms and cold. And moreover, that the army had no other provision to trust unto or depend upon; that he knew that Plymouth forces had not so much as one biscuit left, for he had seen their last dealt out.

The General, advising a few words with the gentlemen that were about him, moved toward the fort, designing to ride in himself and bring in the whole army. But just as he was entering the swamp, one of his captains met him and asked him whither he was going? He told him into the fort. The Captain laid hold of his horse and told him his life was worth an hundred of theirs and he should not expose himself. The General told him that he supposed the brunt was over and that Mr. Church had informed him that the fort was taken. And, as the case was circumstanced, he was of the mind that it was most practicable for him and his army to shelter themselves in the fort. The Captain, in a great heat, replied that Church lied and told the General that if he moved another step towards the fort he would shoot his horse under him.

Then bustled up another gentleman, a certain doctor, and opposed Mr. Church's advice, and said, if it were complied with, it would kill more men than the enemy had killed. For, said he, "by tomorrow the wounded men will be so stiff that there will be no moving of them." And, looking upon Mr. Church and seeing the blood flowing apace from his wounds, told him that if he gave such advice as that was, he should bleed to death like a dog before they would endeavor to staunch his blood. Though after they had prevailed against his advice, they were sufficiently kind to him. And burning up all the houses and provisions in the fort, the army returned the same night in the storm and cold.

And I suppose everyone that is acquainted with the circumstances of that night's march deeply laments the miseries that attended them, especially the wounded and dying men. But it mercifully came to pass that Captain Andrew Belcher arrived at Mr. Smith's that very night from Boston with a vessel loaded with provisions for the army, who must otherwise have perished for want. Some of the enemy that were then in the fort have since informed us that nearly a third of the Indians belonging to all that Narraganset country were killed by the English and by the cold that night; that they fled out of their fort so hastily that they carried nothing with them; that if the English had kept in the fort, the Indians had certainly been necessitated either to surrender themselves to them or to have perished by hunger and the severity of the season.[1]

Some time after this fort fight, a certain Sogkonate Indian, hearing Mr. Church relate the manner of his being wounded, told him that he did not know but he himself was the Indian that wounded him, for that he was one of that company of Indians that Mr. Church made a shot upon when they were rising up to make a shot into the fort; they were in number about 60 or 70, that just then came down from Pumham's town, and never before then fired a gun against the English; that when Mr. Church fired upon them, he killed 14 dead on the spot and wounded a greater number than he killed, many of which died afterwards with their wounds, in the cold and storm the following night.

Mr. Church was moved with other wounded men over to Rhode Island, where in about a month's time he was in some good measure recovered of his wounds and the fever that attended them. And then went over to the General to take his leave of him, with a design to return home.

In the Nipmuck Country

But the General's great importunity again persuaded him to accompany him in a long march into the Nipmuck country, though he had then tents in his wounds, and [was] so lame as not [to be] able to mount his horse without two men's assistance.

In this march the first thing remarkable was [that] they came to an Indian town[1] where there were many wigwams in sight, but an icy swamp lying between them and the wigwams prevented their running at once upon it, as they intended. There was much firing upon each side before they passed the swamp. But, at length, the enemy all fled, and a certain Moohegan that was a friend-Indian, pursued and seized one of the enemy that had a small wound in his leg and brought him before the General, where he was examined. Some were for torturing of him to bring him to a more ample confession of what he knew concerning his countrymen. Mr. Church, verily believing he had been ingenuous in his confession, interceded and prevailed for his escaping torture. But the army being bound forward in their march, and the Indian's wound somewhat disenabling him for travelling, 'twas concluded he should be knocked on the head. Accordingly, he was brought before a great fire, and the Moohegan that took him was allowed, as he desired, to be the executioner.

Mr. Church, taking no delight in the sport, framed an errand at some distance among the baggage horses, and when he had got some ten rods or thereabouts from the fire, the executioner, fetching a blow with his hatchet at the head of the prisoner, he, being aware of the blow, dodged his aside, and the executioner, missing his stroke, the hatchet flew out of his hand and had like to have done execution where 'twas not designed.

The prisoner, upon his narrow escape, broke from them that held him and, notwithstanding his wound, made use of his legs and happened to run right upon Mr. Church, who laid hold on him. And a close scuffle they had; but the Indian, having no clothes on, slipped from him and ran again. And Mr. Church pursued the Indian, although, being lame, there was no great odds in the race, until the Indian stumbled and fell, and they closed again, scuffled, and fought pretty smartly until the Indian, by the advantage of his nakedness, slipped from his hold again and set out on his third race, with Mr. Church close at his heels, endeavoring to lay hold on the hair of his head, which was all the hold could be taken of him. And, running through a swamp that was covered with hollow ice, it made so loud a noise that Mr. Church expected (but in vain) that some of his English friends would follow the noise and come to his assistance.

But the Indian hap't to run athwart a mighty tree that lay fallen near breast-high, where he stopped and cried out aloud for help. But Mr. Church, being soon upon him again, the Indian seized him fast by the hair of his head and, endeavored, by twisting, to break his neck. But, though Mr. Church's wounds had somewhat weakened him, and the Indian [was] a stout fellow, yet he held him well in play and twisted the Indian's neck as well and took the advantage of many opportunities while they hung by each other's hair, to give him notorious bunts in the face with his head.

But in the heat of this scuffle they heard the ice break with some bodies coming apace to them, which, when they heard, Church concluded there was help for one or other of them, but was doubtful which of them must now receive the fatal stroke. Anon, somebody comes up to them who proved to be the Indian that had first taken the prisoner. Without speaking a word, he felt them out (for 'twas so dark he could not distinguish them by sight), the one being clothed, and the other naked; he felt where Mr. Church's hands were fastened in the Netop's[2] hair, and, with one blow, settled his hatchet in between them and ended the strife. He then spoke to Mr. Church and hugged him in his arms and thanked him abundantly for catching his prisoner; and cut off the head of his victim and carried it to the camp. And giving an account to the rest of the friend-Indians in the camp how Mr. Church had seized his prisoner, they all joined a mighty shout.

Proceeding in this march, they had the success of killing many of the enemy, until at length, their provision failing, they returned home.[3]

Philip's Movements and Church's Counsel

King Philip (as was before hinted) was fled to a place called Scattacook, between York and Albany, where the Moohags made a descent upon him and killed many of his men, which moved him from thence.[1]

His next kennelling place was at the falls of Connecticut River, where sometime after Captain Turner found him, came upon him by night, killed him a great many men and frightened many more into the river, that were hurled down the falls and drowned.[2]

Philip got over the river, and on the back side of the Wetuset Hills[3] meets with all the remnants of the Narraganset and Nipmuck Indians, that were there gathered together, and became very numerous; and made their descent on Sudbury and the adjacent parts of the country, where they met with and swallowed up valiant Captain Wadsworth and his company, and [wrought] many other doleful desolations in those parts.

The news whereof coming to Plymouth, and they expecting probably the enemy would soon return again into their colony, the Council of War[4] was called together, and Mr. Church was sent for to them, being observed by the whole colony to be a person extraordinarily qualified for and adapted to the affairs of war. 'Twas proposed in Council that, lest the enemy in their return should fall on Rehoboth, or some other of their out-towns, a company consisting of 60 or 70 men should be sent into those parts, and Mr. Church invited to take the command of them. He told them that if the enemy returned into the colony again, they might reasonably expect that they would come very numerous; and that if he should take the command of men, he should not lie in any town or garrison with them, but would lie in the woods as the enemy did. And that to send out such small companies against such multitudes of the enemy that were now mustered together would be but to deliver so many men into their hands to be destroyed, as the worthy Captain Wadsworth and his company were. His advice, upon the whole, was that if they sent out any forces, to send not less than 300 soldiers, and that the other colonies should be asked to send out their quotas also, adding that, if they intended to make an end of the war by subduing the enemy, they must make a business of the war, as the enemy did; and that, for his own part, he had wholly laid aside all his own private business and concerns ever since the war broke out. He told them that if they would send forth such forces as he should direct to, he would go with them for six weeks' march, which was long enough for men to be kept in the woods at once; and if they might be sure of liberty to return in such a space, men would go out cheerfully. And he would engage 150 of the best soldiers should immediately [en]list voluntarily to go with him if they would please to add 50 more, and 100 of the friend-Indians. And, with such an army, he made no doubt but he might do good service; but on other terms he did not incline to be concerned.

Their reply was that they were already in debt, and so big an army would bring such charge upon them that they should never be able to pay. And as for sending out Indians, they thought it no ways advisable and, in short, none of his advice practicable.

Interlude in Rhode Island

Now Mr. Church's consort and his then only son were till this time remaining at Duxborough, and, his fearing [for] their safety there (unless the war were more vigorously engaged in) [he] resolved to move to Rhode Island, though it was much opposed both by the Government and by relations. But, at length, the Governor, considering that he might be no less serviceable by being on that side of the colony, gave his permit, and wished he had twenty more as good men to send with him.

Then, preparing for his removal, he went with his small family to Plymouth to take leave of their friends, where they met with his wife's parents, who much persuaded that she might be left at Mr. Clark's garrison[1] (which they supposed to be a mighty safe place), or, at least, that she might be there until her soon expected lying-in was over (being near her time). Mr. Church no ways inclining to venture her any longer in those parts, and no arguments prevailing with him, he resolutely set out for Taunton, and many of their friends accompanied them. There they found Captain Peirce,[2] with a commanded party, who offered Mr. Church to send a relation of his with some others to guard him to Rhode Island. But Mr. Church thanked him for his respectful offer, but for some good reasons refused to accept it. In short, they got safe to Captain John Almy's house upon Rhode Island, where they met with friends and good entertainment. But, by the way, let me not forget this remarkable providence: viz, that within twenty-four hours, or thereabouts, after their arrival at Rhode Island, Mr. Clark's garrison that Mr. Church was so much importuned to leave his wife and child at, was destroyed by the enemy.[3]

Mr. Church, being at present disenabled from any particular service in the war, began to think of some other employ; but he no sooner took a tool to cut a small stick, but he cut off the top of his forefinger, and the next to it, half off; upon which he smilingly said that he thought he was out of his way, to leave the war, and resolved he would to war again. Accordingly, his second son being born on the 12th of May,[4] and his wife and son like[ly] to do well, Mr. Church embraces the opportunity of a passage in a sloop bound to Barnstable; who landed him at Sogkonesset,[5] from whence he rode to Plymouth; arrived there on the first Tuesday in June.[6]

Adoption of the Church Strategy

The General Court, then sitting, welcomed him, told him they were glad to see him alive. He replied, he was as glad to see them alive, for he had seen so many fires and smokes towards their side of the country since he left them, that he could scarce eat or sleep with any comfort, for fear they had been all destroyed. For all travelling was stopped, and no news had passed for a long time together. He gave them account, that the Indians had made horrid desolations at Providence,[1] Warwick, Petuxit, and all over the Narraganset country, and that they prevailed daily against the English on that side of the country. Told them he longed to hear what methods they designed in the war. They told him they were particularly glad that Providence had brought him there at that juncture, for they had concluded the very next day to send out an army of 200 men, two thirds English, one third Indians, in some measure agreeable to his former proposal, expecting Boston and Connecticut to join with their quotas.

In short, it was so concluded. And that Mr. Church should return to the Island and see what he could muster there, of those that had moved from Swanzey, Dartmouth, etc. So, returning the same way he came, when he came to Sogkonesset, he had a sham put upon him about a boat he had bought to go home in; and was forced to hire two of the friend-Indians to paddle him in a canoe from Elsabeths to Rhode Island.[2]

It fell out that as they were in their voyage passing by Sogkonate-point, some of the enemy were upon the rocks a-fishing. He bid the Indians that managed the canoe to paddle so near to the rocks as that he might call to those Indians, told them that he had a great mind ever since the war broke out to speak with some of the Sogkonate Indians, and that they were their relations and therefore they need not fear their hurting of them. And, he added that he had a mighty conceit that if he could gain a fair opportunity to discourse [with] them that he could draw them off from Philip, for he knew they never heartily loved him.

The enemy hallooed and made signs for the canoe to come to them. But when they approached them, they skulked and hid in the clefts of the rocks. Then Mr. Church ordered the canoe to be paddled off again, lest if he came too near they should fire upon him. Then, the Indians appearing again, beckoned and called in the Indian language and bid them come ashore; they wanted to speak with them. The Indians in the canoe answered them again; but they on the rocks told them that the surf made such a noise against the rocks, they could not hear anything they said. Then Mr. Church, by signs with his hands, gave to understand that he would have two of them go down upon the point of the beach (a place where a man might see who was near him). Accordingly, two of them ran along the beach and met him there, without their arms, excepting that one of them had a lance in his hand. They urged Mr. Church to come ashore for they had a great desire to have some discourse with him. He told them, if he that had his weapon in his hand would carry it up some distance upon the beach and leave it, he would come ashore and discourse [with] them. He did so, and Mr. Church went ashore, hauled up his canoe, ordered one of his Indians to stay by it, and the other to walk above on the beach as a sentinel to see that the coasts were clear.

Indians Fishing.

Treaty Rock, Little Compton.

Meeting on Sakonnet Point

And, when Mr. Church came up to the Indians, one of them happened to be Honest George, one of the two that Awashonks formerly sent to call him to her dance and was so careful to guard him back to his house again; the last Sogkonate Indian he spoke with before the war broke out; he spoke English very well. Mr. Church asked him where Awashonks was. He told him in a swamp about three miles off.[1] Mr. Church again asked him, what it was he wanted that he hallooed and called him ashore? He answered that he took him for Church as soon as he heard his voice in the canoe, and that he was very glad to see him alive, and he believed his mistress would be as glad to see him, and speak with him. He told him further that he believed she was not fond of maintaining a war with the English, and that she had left Philip and did not intend to return to him any more. He was mighty earnest with Mr. Church to tarry there while he would run and call her, but he told him no, for he did not know but the Indians would come down and kill him before he could get back again. He said, if Mount-hope or Pocasset Indians could catch him, he believed they would knock him on the head. But all Sogkonate Indians knew him very well, and he believed would none of them hurt him. In short, Mr. Church refused then to tarry, but promised that he would come over again and speak with Awashonks and some other Indians that he had a mind to talk with.

Accordingly, he appointed him to notify Awashonks, her son, Peter, their chief captain, and one Nompash[2] (an Indian that Mr. Church had formerly a particular respect for) to meet him two days after at a rock at the lower end of Captain Richmond's farm, which was a very noted place,[3] and, if that day should prove stormy or windy, they were to expect him the next moderate day. Mr. Church telling George that he would have him come with the persons mentioned, and no more. They, giving each other their hand upon it, parted, and Mr. Church went home,[4] and the next morning [went] to Newport and informed the Government what had passed between him and the Sogkonate Indians. And desired their permit for him and Daniel Wilcock (a man that well understood the Indian language) to go over to them. They told him they thought he was mad, after such service as he had done, and such dangers that he escaped, now to throw away his life; for the rogues would as certainly kill him, as ever he went over; and utterly refused to grant his permit, or to be willing that he should run the risk.

Mr. Church told them that it had ever been in his thoughts since the war broke out, that if he could discourse [with] the Sogkonate Indians, he could draw them off from Philip, and employ them against him; but could, till now, never have an opportunity to speak with any of them, and was very loath to lose it. At length, they told him, if he would go, it should be only with the two Indians that came with him;[5] but they would give him no permit under their hands. He took his leave of them, resolving to prosecute his design. They told him they were sorry to see him so resolute, nor if he went did they ever expect to see his face again.

Parley at Treaty Rock

He bought a bottle of rum and a small roll of tobacco to carry with him, and returned to his family, The next morning, being the day appointed for the meeting, he prepared two light canoes for the design, and his own man, with the two Indians for his company. He used such arguments with his tender and now almost broken-hearted wife, from the experience of former preservations, and the prospect of the great service he might do, might it please God to succeed his design, that he obtained her consent to his attempt And, committing her, his babes and himself to Heaven's protection, he set out.

They had from the shore about a league to paddle. Drawing near the place, they saw the Indians sitting on the bank, waiting for their coming. Mr. Church sent one of the Indians ashore in one of the canoes to see whether it were the same Indians whom he had appointed to meet him, and no more; and, if so, to stay ashore and send George to fetch him. Accordingly, George came and fetched Mr. Church ashore, while the other canoe played off to see the event and to carry tidings if the Indians should prove false.

Mr. Church asked George whether Awashonks and the other Indians he appointed to meet him were there. He answered they were. He then asked him if there were no more than they whom he appointed to be there? To which he would give him no direct answer. However, he went ashore, where he was no sooner landed but Awashonks and the rest that he had appointed to meet him there, rose up and came down to meet him; and each of them successively gave him their hands, and expressed themselves glad to see him, and gave him thanks for exposing himself to visit them. They walked together about a gun shot from the water to a convenient place to sit down. Where at once arose up a great body of Indians who had lain hid in the grass (that was as high as a man's waist) and gathered round them till they had closed them in, being all armed with guns, spears, hatchets, etc., with their hair trimmed and faces painted in their warlike appearance. It was doubtless somewhat surprising to our gentleman at first, but, without any visible discovery of it, after a small silent pause on each side, he spoke to Awashonks and told her that George had informed him that she had a desire to see him and discourse about making peace with the English.

She answered, Yes.

"Then," said Mr. Church, "it is customary when people meet to treat of peace, to lay aside their arms, and not to appear in such hostile form as your people do"; desired of her that if they might talk about peace, which he desired they might, her men might lay aside their arms and appear more treatable. Upon which there began a considerable noise and murmur among them in their own language. Till Awashonks asked him what arms they should lay down, and where? He (perceiving the Indians looked very surly and much displeased) replied, "Only their guns at some small distance, for formality's sake." Upon which, with one consent, they laid aside their guns and came and sat down.

Mr. Church pulled out his calabash and asked Awashonks whether she had lived so long at Wetuset as to forget to drink occapechees;[1] and, drinking to her, he perceived that she watched him very diligently, to see (as he thought) whether he swallowed any of the rum. He offered her the shell, but she desired him to drink again first. He then told her, there was no poison in it, and pouring some into the palm of his hand, supped it up, and took the shell and drank to her again, and drank a good swig, which, indeed, was no more than he needed. Then, they all standing up, he said to Awashonks:

"You won't drink for fear there should be poison in it."

And then handed it to a little ill-looked fellow, who catched it readily enough, and as greedily would have swallowed the liquor when he had it at his mouth. But Mr. Church catched him by the throat and took it from him, asking him whether he intended to swallow shell and all? And then handed it to Awashonks. She ventured to take a good hearty dram, and passed it among her attendants.

The shell being emptied, he pulled out his tobacco, and having distributed it, they began to talk.

Awashonks demanded of him the reason why he had not (agreeable to his promise when she saw him last) been down at Sogkonate before now, saying that probably if he had come then according to his promise, they had never joined with Philip against the English.

He told her he was prevented by the war's breaking out so suddenly. And yet, he was afterwards coming down, and came as far as Punkateese, where a great many Indians set upon him and fought him a whole afternoon, though he did not come prepared to fight, had but nineteen men with him, whose chief design was to gain a[n] opportunity to discourse [with] some Sogkonate Indians. Upon this, there at once arose a mighty murmur, confused noise, and talk among the fierce-looked creatures, and all rising up in a hubbub; and a great surly-looked fellow took up his tomhog or wooden cutlass to kill Mr. Church, but some others prevented him.

The interpreter asked Mr. Church if he understood what it was that the great fellow (they had hold of) said. He answered him, No.

"Why," said the interpreter, "he says you killed his brother at Punkateese and therefore he thirsts for your blood."

Mr. Church bid the interpreter tell him that his brother began first, that if he had kept at Sogkonate according to his desire and order, he should not have hurt him.

Then the chief Captain commanded "Silence," and told them they should talk no more about old things, and quelled the tumult so that they sat down again and began upon a discourse of making peace with the English. Mr. Church asked them what proposals they would make and on what terms they would break their league with Philip. Desiring them to make some proposals that he might carry to his masters, telling them that it was not in his power to conclude a peace with them, but that he knew that if their proposals were reasonable, the Government would not be unreasonable, and that he would use his interest in the Government for them. And to encourage them to proceed, put them in mind that the Pequots once made war with the English and that after they subjected themselves to the English, the English became their protectors and defended them against other nations that would otherwise have destroyed them. After some further discourse and debate, he brought them at length to consent that if the Government of Plymouth would firmly engage to them, that they and all of them, and their wives and children should have their lives spared, and none of them transported out of the country, they would subject themselves to them, and serve them in what they were able.

Then Mr. Church told them that he was well satisfied the Government of Plymouth would readily concur with what they proposed, and would sign their articles. And, complimenting them upon it, how pleased he was with the thoughts of their return and of the former friendship that had been between them.

The chief Captain rose up and expressed the great value and respect he had for Mr. Church; and, bowing to him, said,

"Sir, if you'll please to accept of me and my men and will head us, we'll fight for you and will help you to Philip's head before Indian corn be ripe."

And when he had ended, they all expressed their consent to what he said, and told Mr. Church they loved him and were willing to go with him and fight for him as long as the English had one enemy left in the country.

Mr. Church assured them that if they proved as good as their word, they should find him theirs and their children's fast friend. And (by the way), the friendship is maintained between them to this day.

Then he proposed unto them, that they should choose five men to go straight with him to Plymouth. They told him, no; they would not choose, but he should take which five he pleased. Some compliments passed about it; at length, it was agreed they should choose three, and he, two. Then he agreed with that he would go back to the Island that night, and would come to them the next morning and go through the woods to Plymouth. But they afterwards objected that this travelling through the woods would not be safe for him; the enemy might meet with them and kill him, and then they should lose their friend, and the whole design ruined beside. And therefore proposed that he should come in an English vessel, and they would meet him and come on board at Sogkonate-point, and sail from thence to Sandwich; which, in fine, was concluded upon.

So Mr. Church, promising to come as soon as he could possibly obtain a vessel, and then they parted. He returned to the Island and was at great pains and charge to get a vessel, but with unaccountable disappointments, sometimes by the falseness, and sometimes by the faint-heartedness of men that he bargained with, and something by wind and weather.

Until at length Mr. Anthony Low put into the harbor with a laden vessel bound to the westward, and, being made acquainted with Mr. Church's case, told him that he had so much kindness for him and was so pleased with the business that he engaged in, that he would run the venture of his vessel and cargo to wait upon him. Accordingly, next morning they set sail with a wind that soon brought them to Sogkonate-point; but, coming there, they met with a contrary wind and a great swelling sea.

The Indians were there waiting upon the rocks, but had nothing but a miserable broken canoe to get aboard in. Yet Peter Awashonks ventured off in it, and, with a great deal of difficulty and danger, got aboard. And by this time it began to rain and blow exceedingly and forced them away up the sound; and then went away through Bristol Ferry, round the Island to Newport, carrying Peter with them.

Then Mr. Church dismissed Mr. Low and told him that, inasmuch as Providence opposed his going by water, and he expected that the army would be up in a few days, and probably if he should be gone at that juncture it might ruin the whole design, [he] would therefore yield his voyage.

Then he writ the account of his transactions with the Indians and drew up the proposals and articles of peace, and dispatched Peter with them to Plymouth, that His Honour the Governor, if he saw cause, might sign them.

Peter was set over to Sogkonate on the Lord's Day morning,[2] with orders to take those men that were chosen to go down, or some of them at least, with him. The time being expired that was appointed for the English army to come, there was great looking for them. Mr. Church on the Monday morning (partly to divert himself after his fatigue, and partly to listen for the army) rode out with his wife and some of his friends to Portsmouth, under a pretense of cherrying; but came home without any news from the army. But by midnight, or sooner, he was roused with an express from Major Bradford, who was arrived with the army at Pocasset. To whom he forthwith repaired,[3] and informed him of the whole of his proceedings with the Sogkonate Indians.

With the Major's consent and advice, he returned again next morning to the Island in order to go over that way to Awashonks, to inform her that the army was arrived. Accordingly, from Sachueeset-Neck[4] he went in a canoe to Sogkonate; told her Major Bradford was arrived at Pocasset, with a great army, whom he had informed of all his proceedings with her. That if she would be advised and observe order, she nor her people need not to fear being hurt by them. Told her, she should call all her people down into the neck, lest if they should be found straggling about, mischief might light on them. That on the morrow they would come down and receive her, and give her further orders. She promised to get as many of her people together as possibly she could. Desiring Mr. Church to consider that it would be difficult for to get them together at such short warning.

Mr. Church returned to the Island and to the army the same night. The next morning the whole army marched towards Sogkonate as far as Punkateese; and Mr. Church with a few men went down to Sogkonate to call Awashonks and her people to come up to the English camp. As he was going down, they met with a Pocasset Indian who had killed a cow and got a quarter of her on his back, and her tongue in his pocket; who gave them an account, that he came from Pocasset two days since in company with his mother and several other Indians now hid in a swamp above Nomquid.[5] Disarming of him, he sent him by two men to Major Bradford, and proceeded to Sogkonate. They saw Indians by the way skulking about, but let them pass.

Submission of Awashonks at Punkatees

Arriving at Awashonk's camp, told her, he was come to invite her and her people up to Punkateese, where Major Bradford now was with the Plymouth army, expecting her and her subjects to receive orders, until further order could be had from the Government. She complied, and soon sent out orders for such of her subjects as were not with her, immediately to come in. And by twelve o'clock of the next day, she, with most of her number, appeared before the English camp at Punkateese.[1] Mr. Church tendered the Major to serve under his commission, provided the Indians might be accepted with him, to fight the enemy. The Major told him, his orders were to improve him, if pleased, but as for the Indians, he would not be concerned with them. And presently gave forth orders for Awashonks and all her subjects, both men, women and children, to repair to Sandwich, and to be there, upon peril, in six days.

Awashonks and her chiefs gathered round Mr. Church (where he was walked off from the rest), expressed themselves concerned that they could not be confided in, nor improved. He told them 'twas best to obey orders, and that if he could not accompany them to Sandwich, it should not be above a week before he would meet them there; that he was confident the Governor would commission him to improve them. The Major hastened to send them away with Jack Havens (an Indian who had never been in the wars) in the front with a flag of truce in his hand. They being gone, Mr. Church, by the help of his man Toby (the Indian whom he had taken prisoner as he was going down to Sogkonate), took said Toby's mother,[2] and those that were with her prisoners. Next morning, the whole army moved back to Pocasset. This Toby informed them that there were a great many Indians gone down to Wepoiset[3] to eat clams (other provisions being very scarce with them); that Philip himself was expected within 3 or 4 days at the same place. Being asked what Indians they were, he answered, "Some Weetemore's Indians, some Mount-hope Indians, some Narraganset Indians, and some other upland Indians, in all about 300."

The Rhode Island boats, by the Major's order, meeting them at Pocasset, they were soon embarked, it being just in the dusk of the evening, they could plainly discover the enemy's fires at the place the Indian directed to. And the army concluded no other but they were bound directly thither, until they came to the north end of the Island and heard the word of command for the boats to bear away. Mr. Church was very fond of having this probable opportunity of surprising that whole company of Indians embraced. But orders, 'twas said, must be obeyed, which was to go to Mount-hope and there to fight Philip. This, with some other good opportunities of doing spoil upon the enemy being unhappily missed, Mr. Church obtained the Major's consent to meet the Sogkonate Indians according to his promise. He was offered a guard to Plymouth, but chose to go with one man only, who was a good pilot. About sunset[4] he, with Sabin his pilot, mounted their horses at Rehoboth, where the army now was, and by two hours by sun next morning arrived safe at Plymouth.

And by that time they had refreshed themselves, the Governor and Treasurer came to town. Mr. Church, giving them a short account of the affairs of the army, His Honor was pleased to give him thanks for the good and great

Penelope Winslow, Wife of Governor Winslow.

Josiah Winslow, Governor of Plymouth.

service he had done at Sogkonate, told him, he had confirmed all that he promised Awashonks, and had sent the Indian back again that brought his letter. He asked His Honor whether he had anything later from Awashonks. He told him he had not. Whereupon he gave His Honor account of the Major's orders relating to her and hers, and what discourse had passed pro and con about them; and that he had promised to meet them, and that he had encouraged them, that he thought he might obtain of his Honor a commission to lead them forth to fight Philip.

His Honor smilingly told him, that he should not want commission if he would accept it, nor yet good Englishmen enough to make up a good army. But, in short, he told His Honor the time was expired that he had appointed to meet the Sogkonates at Sandwich.

The Governor asked him when he would go? He told him that afternoon, by His Honor's leave. The governor asked him how many men he would have with him? He answered, not above half a dozen, with an order to take more at Sandwich if he saw cause and horses provided. He no sooner moved it, but had his number of men tendering to go with him, among which was Mr. Jabez Howland, and Nathaniel Southworth. They went to Sandwich that night, where Mr. Church (with need enough) took a nap of sleep. The next morning, with about 16 or 18 men, proceeded as far as Agawom,[5] where they had great expectation of meeting the Indians, but met them not. His men, being discouraged, about half of them returned; only half-a-dozen stuck by him and promised so to do until they should meet with the Indians. When they came to Sippican River,[6] Mr. Howland began to tire, upon which Mr. Church left him and two more, for a reserve at the river, that, if he should meet with enemies and be forced back, they might be ready to assist them in getting over the river. Proceeding in their march, they crossed another river and opened a great bay, where they might see many miles alongshore, where were sands and flats.[7] And, hearing a great noise below them towards the sea, they dismounted their horses, left them, and crept among the bushes until they came near the bank and saw a vast company of Indians, of all ages and sexes, some on horseback running races, some at football, some catching eels and flat fish in the water, some clamming, but which way with safety to find out what Indians they were, they were at a loss.

Reunion with Awashonks

But, at length, retiring into a thicket, Mr. Church halooed to them. They soon answered him, and a couple of smart young fellows, well-mounted, came upon a full career to see who it might be that called, and came just upon Mr. Church before they discovered him. But, when they perceived themselves so near Englishmen, and armed, were much surprised, and tacked short about to run as fast back as they came forward, until one of the men in the bushes called to them, and told them his name was Church, and need not fear his hurting of them. Upon which, after a small pause, they turned about their horses and came up to him. One of them that could speak English, Mr. Church took aside and examined, who informed him that the Indians below were Awashonks and her company, and that Jack Havens was among them, whom Mr. Church immediately sent for to come to him, and ordered the messenger to inform Awashonks that he was come to meet her. Jack Havens soon came, and by that time Mr. Church had asked him a few questions, and had been satisfied by him, that it was Awashonks and her company that were below, and that Jack had been kindly treated by them, a company of Indians, all mounted on horseback and well armed, came riding up to Mr. Church, but treated him with all due respect. He then ordered Jack to go tell Awashonks that he designed to sup with her in the evening and to lodge in her camp that night.

Then, taking some of the Indians with him, he went back to the river to take care of Mr. Howland. Mr. Church, being a mind to try what metal he was made of, imparted his notion to the Indians that were with him and gave them directions how to act their parts. When he came pretty near the place, he and his Englishmen pretendedly fled, firing on their retreat towards the Indians that pursued them, and they firing as fast after them. Mr. Howland, being upon his guard, hearing the guns, and by and by seeing the motion both of the English and Indians, concluded his friends were distressed, was soon on the full career on horseback to meet them, until he, perceiving their laughing, mistrusted the truth. As soon as Mr. Church had given him the news, they hasted away to Awashonks.

Upon their arrival, they were immediately conducted to a shelter, open on one side, whither Awashonks and her chiefs soon came and paid their respects. And the multitudes gave shouts as made the heavens to ring. It being now about sunsetting, or near the dusk of the evening, the Netops came running from all quarters laden with the tops of dry pines and the like combustible matter, making a huge pile thereof near Mr. Church's shelter, on the open side thereof. But by this time supper was brought in, in three dishes; viz., a curious young bass in one dish, eels and flat fish in a second, and shell fish in a third, but neither bread nor salt to be seen at table.

But by that time supper was over, the mighty pile of pine knots and tops was fired, and all the Indians great and small gathered in a ring around it. Awashonks with the oldest of her people, men and women mixed, kneeling down, made the first ring next the fire, and all the lusty stout men standing up made the next; and then all the rabble in a confused crew surrounded on the outside. Then the chief Captain stepped in between the rings and the fire, with a spear in one hand and a hatchet in the other, danced round the fire, and began to fight with it, making mention of all the several nations and companies of Indians in the country that were enemies to the English. And, at naming of every particular tribe of Indians, he would draw out and fight a new fire-brand, and at his finishing his fight with each particular fire-brand, would bow to him and thank him. And, when he had named all the several nations and tribes, and fought them all, he stuck down his spear and hatchet, and came out; and another stepped in and acted over the same dance, with more fury, if possible, than the first. And, when about half-a-dozen of their chiefs had thus acted their parts, the Captain of the Guard stepped up to Mr. Church and told him they were making soldiers for him, and what they had been doing was all one swearing of them, and, having in that manner engaged all the lusty stout men. Awashonks and her chiefs came to Mr. Church and told him that now they were all engaged to fight for the English, and he might call forth all, or any of them at any time as he saw occasion to fight the enemy. And presented him with a very fine firelock.

Mr. Church accepts their offer, drew out a number of them, and set out next morning before day for Plymouth, where they arrived safe the same day.

A New Commission

The Governor being informed of it, came early to town next morning. And by the time he had Englishmen enough to make up a good company, when joined with Mr. Church's Indians, that offered their voluntary service to go under his command in quest of the enemy. The Governor then gave him a Commission, which is as follows:

Captain Benjamin Church, *you are hereby Nominated, Ordered, Commission'd and Impowred to raise a Company of Volunteers of about 200 Men,* English *and* Indians: *the English not exceeding the number of 60, of which Company, or so many of them as you can obtain, or shall see cause at present to improve, you are to take the command and conduct, and to lead them forth now and hereafter, at such time, and unto such places within this Colony, or else where, within the confederate Colonies, as you shall think fit; to discover, pursue, fight, surprize, destroy, or subdue our* Indian *Enemies, or any part or parties of them that by the Providence of God you may meet with; or them or any of them by treaty and composition to receive to mercy, if you see reason (provided they be not Murderous Rogues, or such as have been principal Actors in those Villanies:) And forasmuch as your Company may be uncertain, and the Persons often changed, You are also hereby impowred with advice of your Company to chuse and Commissionate a Lieutenant, and to establish Serjeants, and Corporals as you see cause: And you herein improving your best judgment and discretion and utmost ability, faithfully to Serve the Interest of God, His Majesty's Interest, and the Interest of the Colony; and carefully govern-*

ing your said Company at home and abroad: these shall be unto you full and ample Commission, Warrant and Discharge. Given under the Publick Seal, this 24th Day of July 1676.[1]

Per Jos. Winslow, GOV.

Running Down the Enemy

Receiving commission, he marched the same night into the woods, got to Middleberry[1] before day, and, as soon as the light appeared, took into the woods and swampy thickets towards a place where they had some reason to expect to meet with a parcel of Narraganset Indians, with some others that belonged to Mount-hope. Coming near to where they expected them, Captain Church's Indian scout discovered the enemy, and, well observing their fires, and postures, returned with the intelligence to their Captain, who gave such directions for the surrounding of them as had the direct effect, surprising them from every side so unexpectedly that they were all taken. Not so much as one escaped. And, upon a strict examination, they gave intelligence of another parcel of the enemy at a place called Munponset Pond. Captain Church hastening with his prisoners through the woods to Plymouth, disposed of them all, excepting only one, Jeffery, who, proving very ingenious and faithful to him, in informing where other parcels of the Indians harbored, Captain Church promised him that, if he continued to be faithful to him, he should not be sold out of the country, but should be his waiting man, to take care of his horse, etc., and, accordingly, he served him faithfully as long as he lived.

But Captain Church was forthwith sent out again; and the terms for his encouragement being concluded on, viz., that the country should find them ammunition and provision, and have half the prisoners and arms they took, the Captain and his English soldiers to have the other half of the prisoners and arms; and the Indian soldiers the loose plunder. Poor encouragement! But after some time it was mended.

They soon captivated [sic] the Munponsets and brought in, not one escaping. This stroke he held several weeks, never returning empty handed. When he wanted intelligence of their kennelling places, he would march to some place likely to meet with some travellers or ramblers, and, scattering his company, would lie close, and seldom lay above a day or two, at the most, before some of them would fall into their hands, whom he would compel to inform where their company was. And so, by his method of secret and sudden surprises, took great numbers of them prisoners.

The Government, observing his extraordinary courage and conduct, and the success from Heaven added to it, saw cause to enlarge his commission; gave him power to raise and dismiss his forces, as he should see occasion; to commissionate officers under him, and to march as far as he should see cause, within the limits of the three United Colonies, to receive to mercy, give quarter, or not; excepting some particular and noted murderers: viz., Philip, and all that were at the destroying of Mr. Clark's garrison, and some few others.

Major Bradford, being now at Taunton with his army and wanting provisions, some carts were ordered from Plymouth for their supply, and Captain Church to guard them.[2] But he, obtaining other guards for the carts, as far as Middleborough, ran before with a small company, hoping to meet with some of the enemy, appointing the carts and their guards to meet them at Nemascut about an hour after the sun's rising next morning. He arrived there about the breaking of the daylight, discovered a company of the enemy, but his time was too short to wait for gaining advantage, and therefore ran right in upon them, surprised and captivated about 16 of them, who, upon examination, informed, that Tispaquin,[3] a very famous captain among the enemy, was at Assawompset with a numerous company.

But the carts must now be guarded, and the opportunity of visiting Tispaquin must now be laid aside. The carts are to be faithfully guarded, lest Tispaquid [sic] should attack them.

Coming towards Taunton, Captain Church, taking two men with him, made all speed to the town. And, coming to the riverside, he hallooed, and, inquiring of them that came to the river, for Major Bradford or his captains, he was informed they were in the town, at the tavern. He told them of the carts that were coming, that he had the cumber of guarding of them, which had already prevented his improving opportunities of doing service. Prayed, therefore, that a guard might be sent over to receive the carts, that he might be at liberty, refusing all invitations and persuasions, to go over to the tavern, to visit the Major, he at length obtained a guard to receive the carts; by whom also he sent his prisoners to be conveyed with the carts to Plymouth, directing them not to return by the way they came, but by Bridgwater.

Hastening back, he purposed to camp that night at Assawompset Neck. But, as soon as they came to the river that runs into the great pond through the thick swamp at the entering of the neck, the enemy fired upon them, but hurt not a man. Captain Church's Indians ran right into the swamp and fired upon them, but it being in the dusk of the evening, the enemy made their escape in the thickets. The Captain, then moving about a mile into the neck, took the advantage of a small valley to feed his horses. Some held the horses by the bridles; the rest, on the guard, looked sharp out for the enemy, within hearing on every side, and some very near; but in the dead of the night, the enemy being out of hearing, or still, Captain Church moved out of the neck (not the same way he came in, lest he should be ambuscado'd) toward Cushnet, where all the houses were burnt.[4] And, crossing Cushnet River, being extremely fatigued, with two night's and one day's ramble without rest or sleep, and observing good forage for their horses, the Captain concluded upon abating and taking a nap. Setting six men to watch the passage of the river, two to watch at a time, while the other slept, and so to take their turns, while the rest of the company went into a thicket to sleep under the guard of two sentinels more. But the whole company, being very drowsy, soon forgot their danger and were fast asleep, sentinels and all.

Capture of Little Eyes

The Captain first awakes, looks up, and judges he had slept four hours, which, being longer than he designed, immediately rouses his company, and sends away a file to see what were become of the watch at the passage of the river, but they no sooner opened the river in sight, but they discovered a company of the enemy viewing of their tracks, where they came into the neck. Captain Church and those with him soon dispersed into the brush on each side of the way, while the file sent, got undiscovered to the passage of the river and found their watch all fast asleep. But these tidings thoroughly awakened the whole company. But the enemy giving them no present disturbance, they examined their snapsacks and, taking a little refreshment, the Captain orders one party to guard the horses and the other to scout, who soon met with a track, and, following of it, they were brought to a small company of Indians, who proved to be Little Eyes and his family, and near relations, who were at Sogkonate, but had forsaken their countrymen upon their making peace with English. Some of Captain Church's Indians asked him if he did not know that fellow? Told him, "This is the rogue that would have killed you at Awashonk's dance," and signified to him that now he had an opportunity to be revenged on him. But the Captain told them, it was not Englishman's fashion to seek revenge, and that he should have the same quarter the rest had. Moving to the riverside, they found an old canoe, with which the Captain ordered Little Eyes and his company to be carried over to an island.[1] Telling him he would leave him on that island until he returned; and, lest the English should light on them and kill them, he would leave his cousin, Lightfoot[2] (whom the English knew to be their friend) to be his guard. Little Eyes expressed himself very thankful to the Captain.

He, leaving his orders with Light-foot, returns to the riverside toward Poneganset to Russel's orchard. Coming near the orchard, they clapped into a thicket and there lodged the rest of the night without any fire; and, upon the morning light appearing, moves towards the orchard, discovers some of the enemy, who had been there the day before, and had beat down all the apples and carried them away; discovered also where they had lodged that night, and saw the ground where they set their baskets bloody, being as they supposed, and it was afterwards discovered to be, with the flesh of swine, which they had killed that day. They had lain under the fences without any fires, and seemed by the marks they left behind them to be very numerous, perceived also by the dew on the grass that they had not been long gone; and therefore moved apace in pursuit of them.

Raiding in the Great Cedar Swamp

Travelling three miles or more, they came into the country road where the track parted, one parcel steered towards the west end of the Great Cedar Swamp, and the other, to the east end.[1]

The Captain halted and told his Indian soldiers that they had heard as well as he what some had said at Plymouth about them. That now was a good opportunity for each party to prove themselves. The track being divided they should follow one, and the English the other, being equal in number. The Indians declined the motion and were not willing to move anywhere without him; said, they should not think themselves safe without him. But, the Captain insisting upon it, they submitted. He gave the Indians their choice to follow which track they pleased. They replied, they were light and able to travel, therefore, if he pleased, they would take the west track. And, appointing the ruins of John Cook's[2] house at Cushnet for the place to meet at, each company set out briskly to try their fortunes.

Captain Church, with his English soldiers, followed their track until they came near entering a mirey swamp, when the Captain heard a whistle in the rear (which was a note for a halt). Looking behind him, he saw William Fobes[3] start out of the company and made towards him, who hastened to meet him as fast as he could. Fobes told him they had discovered abundance of Indians, and, if he pleased to go a few steps back, he might see them himself.

He did so, and saw them across the swamp. Observing them, he perceived they were gathering of hurtleberries, and that they had no apprehensions of their being so near them. The Captain supposed them to be chiefly women, and, therefore, calling one Mr. Dillano,[4] who was acquainted with the ground and the Indian language, and another named Mr. Barns, with these two men he takes right through the swamp as fast as he could and orders the rest to hasten after them.

Captain Church with Dillano and Burns, having good horses, spurred on and were soon among the thickest of the Indians, and out of sight of their own men. Among the enemy was an Indian woman who, with her husband, had been drove off from Rhode Island notwithstanding they had an house upon Mr. Sanford's[5] land and had planted an orchard before the war, yet the inhabitants would not be satisfied till they were sent off. And Captain Church with his family, living then at the said Sanford's, became acquainted with them, who thought it very hard to turn off such old, quiet people; but in the end it proved a Providence and an advantage to him and his family, as you may see afterwards.

This Indian woman knew Captain Church and, as soon as she saw him, held up both her hands and came running towards him, crying aloud, "Church! Church! Church!"

Captain Church bid her stop the rest of the Indians and tell them, the way to save their lives was not to run but yield themselves prisoners, and he would not kill them. So, with her help and Dillano's, who could call to them in their own language, many of them stopped and surrendered themselves; others scampering and casting away their baskets, betook themselves to the thickets, but Captain Church, being on horseback, soon came up with them and laid hold on a gun that was in the hand of the foremost of the company, pulled it from him, and told him he must go back. And, when he had turned them, he began to look about him to see where he was, and what was become of his company, hoping they might be all as well employed as himself, but could fine none but Dillano, who was very busy gathering up prisoners. The Captain drove his [prisoners] that he had stopped to the rest, inquiring of Dillano for their company, but could have no news of them. But, moving back, picked up now and then a skulking prisoner by the way.

When they came near the place where they first started the Indians, they discovered their company standing in a body together, and had taken some few prisoners. When they saw their Captain, they hastened to meet him. They told him they found it difficult getting through the swamp, and, neither seeing nor hearing anything of him, they concluded the enemy had killed him and were at a great loss what to do. Having brought their prisoners together, they found they had taken and killed 66 of the enemy. Captain Church then asked the old squaw, what company they belonged unto?

Philip and Quinnapin

She said, they belonged to Philip and part to Qunnappin[1] and the Narraganset-Sachem.[2] Discovered also upon her declaration that both Philip and Qunnappin were about two miles off in the great Cedar Swamp.[3] He enquired of her, what company they had with them?

She answered, "Abundance of Indians." The swamp, she said, was full of Indians from one end unto the other, that were settled there, that there were near an 100 men came from the swamp with them and left them upon that plain to gather hurtleberries, and promised to call them as they came back out of Sconticut-Neck,[4] whither they went to kill cattle and horses for provisions for the company. She, perceiving Captain Church move towards the neck, told him, if they went that way, they would all be killed.

He asked her, whereabout they crossed the river?

She pointed to the upper passing place. Upon which Captain Church passed over so low down as he thought it not probable they should meet with his track in their return, and hastened towards the island where he left Little Eyes with Light-foot. Finding a convenient place by the riverside for the securing their prisoners, Captain Church and Mr. Dillano went down to see what was become of Captain Light-foot and the prisoners left in his charge.

Light-foot, seeing and knowing them, soon came over with his broken canoe and informed them that he had seen that day about 100 men of the enemy go down into Sconticut Neck, and that they were now returning again. Upon which, they three ran down immediately to a meadow where Light-foot said the Indians had passed; where they not only saw their tracks, but also them. Whereupon, they lay close until the enemy came into the said meadow and the foremost sat down his load and halted until all the company came up, and then took up their loads and marched again the same way that they came down into the neck, which was the nearest way unto their camp. Had they gone the other way along the river, they could not have missed Captain Church's track, which would doubtless have exposed them to the loss of their prisoners, if not of their lives.

But as soon as the coast was clear of them, the Captain sends his Light-foot to fetch his prisoners from the island, while he and Mr. Dillano returns to the company, sent part of them to conduct Light-foot and his company to the aforesaid meadow, where Captain Church and his company met them.

Crossing the enemy's track, they made all haste until they got over Mattapoiset-river, near about four miles beyond the ruins of Cook's house, where he appointed to meet his Indian company, whither he sent Dillano, with two more, to meet them, ordering them, that, if the Indians were not arrived, to wait for them.

Accordingly, finding no Indians there, they waited until late in the night, when they arrived with their booty. They dispatched a post to their Captain to give him an account of their success; but the day broke before they came to him. And, when they had compared successes, they very remarkably found that the number that each company had taken and slain was equal. The Indians had killed 3 of the enemy and taken 63 prisoners, as the English had done before them. Both English and Indians were surprised at this remarkable Providence, and were both parties rejoicing at it, being both before afraid of what might have been the event of the unequal success of the parties. But the Indians had the fortune to take more arms than the English. They told the Captain that they had missed a brave opportunity by parting. They came upon a great town of the enemy, viz., Captain Tyasks company (Tyasks was the next man to Philip). They fired upon the enemy before they were discovered and ran upon them with a shout. The men ran and left their wives and children, and many of them, their guns. They took Tyasks wife and son and thought that if their Captain and the English company had been with them, they might have taken some hundreds of them. And now they determined not to part anymore.

That night Philip sent (as afterwards they found out) a great army to waylay Captain Church at the entering on of Assawompset Neck, expecting he would have returned the same way he went in. But that was never his method, to return the same way that he came; and, at this time, going another way, he escaped falling into the hands of his enemies. The next day they went home by Scipican, and got well with their prisoners to Plymouth.

Tactics of Indian Warfare

He soon went out again, and this stroke he drove many weeks. And, when he took any number of prisoners, he would pick out some that he took a fancy to, and would tell them, he took a particular fancy to them and had chose them for himself to make soldiers of; and, if any would behave themselves well, he would do well by them and they should be his men and not sold out of the country. If he perceived they looked surly, and his Indian soldiers called them "treacherous dogs," as some of them would sometimes do, all the notice he would take of it would only be to clap them on the back and tell them, "Come, come, you look wild and surly, and mutter, but that signifies nothing. These, my best soldiers were a little while ago as wild and surly as you are now. By that time you have been but one day along with me, you'll love me too, and be as brisk as any of them."

And it proved so. For there was none of them but, after they had been a little while with him, and seen his behavior, and how cheerful and successful his men were, would be as ready to pilot him to any place where the Indians dwelt or haunted (though their own fathers or nearest relations should be among them), or to fight for him, as any of his own men.

Captain Church was in two particulars much advantaged by the great English army[1] that was now abroad. One was, that they drove the enemy down to that part of the country, viz., to the eastward of Taunton River, by which means his business was nearer home. The other was that whenever he fell on with a push upon any body of the enemy (were they never so many), they fled, expecting the great army. And his manner of marching through the woods was such, as if he were discovered, they appeared to be more than they were. For he always marched at a wide distance, one from another, partly for their safety; and this was an Indian custom, to march thin and scatter. Captain Church enquired of some of the Indians that were become his soldiers, how they got such advantage often of the English in their marches through the woods. They told him that the Indians gained great advantage of the English by two things: the Indians always took care in their marches and fights not to come too thick together. But the English always kept in a heap together; that it was as easy to hit them as to hit an house. The other was, that, if any time they discovered a company of English soldiers in the woods, they knew that there was all, for the English never scattered, but the Indians always divided and scattered.

Captain Church, now at Plymouth, something or other happened that kept him at home a few days, until a post came to Marshfield on the Lord's Day morning,[2] informing the Governor that a great army of Indians were discovered, who, it was supposed, were designing to get over the river towards Taunton or Bridgwater, to attack those towns that lay on that side the river. The Governor hastened to Plymouth, raised what men he could by the way, came to Plymouth in the beginning of the forenoon exercise, sent for Captain Church out of the meeting-house, gave him the news, and desired him immediately to rally what of his company he could; and what men he had raised should join them. The Captain bestirs himself, but found no bread in the storehouse and so was forced to run from house to house to get household bread for their march. But this, nor anything else, prevented his marching by the beginning of the afternoon exercise. Marching with what men were ready, he took with him the post that came from Bridgwater to pilot him to the place where he thought he might meet with the enemy.

In the evening[3] they heard a smart firing at a distance from them, but, it being near night, and the firing but of short continuance, they missed the place and went into Bridgwater town. It seems, the occasion of the firing was that Philip, finding that Captain Church made that side of the country too hot for him, designed to return to the other side of the country that he came last from. And, to Taunton River with his company, they felled a great tree across the river for a bridge to pass over on. And, just as Philip's old Uncle Akkompoin[4] and some other of his chiefs were passing over the tree, some brisk Bridgwater lads had ambushed them, fired upon them, and killed the old man and several others, which put a stop to their coming over the river that night.

Next morning,[5] Captain Church moved very early with his company which was increased by many of Bridgwater that listed under him for that expedition; and by their piloting, he soon came very still, to the top of the great tree which the enemy had fallen across the river. And the Captain spied an Indian sitting upon the stump of it on the other side of the river. And he clapped his gun up, and had doubtless dispatched him but that one of his own Indians called hastily to him, not to fire, for he believed it was one of his own men. Upon which, the Indian upon the stump looked about, and Captain Church's Indian, seeing his face, perceived his mistake, for he knew him to be Philip; clapped up his gun and fired, but it was too late, for Philip immediately threw himself off the stump, leapt down a bank on the side of the river, and made his escape.

Capture of Philip's Wife and Son

Captain Church, as soon as possible, got over the river and scattered in quest of Philip and his company; but the enemy scattered and fled every way. But he picked up a considerable many of their women and children, among which was Philip's wife and son, of about nine year's old.[1]

Discovering a considerable new track along the river, and examining the prisoners, [he] found that it was Qunnappin and the Narragansets that were drawing off from those parts towards the Narraganset country. He inquired of the prisoners whether Philip were gone in the same track? They told him they did not know, for he fled in a great fright when the first English gun was fired, and they had none of them seen or heard anything of him since.

Captain Church left part of his company there to secure the prisoners they got and to pick up what more they could find and, with the rest of his company, hasted in the track of the enemy to overtake them, if it might be, before they got over the river, and ran some miles along the river until he came unto a place where the Indians had waded over. And he with his company waded over after them up to the armpits, being almost as wet before with sweat as the river could make them. Following about a mile further, and not overtaking them, and the Captain being under a necessity to return that night to the army, [he] came to an halt, [and] told his company he must return to his other men.

His Indians soldiers moved for leave to pursue the enemy (though he returned); said, the Narragansets were great rogues and they wanted to be revenged on them for killing some of their relations, named Tokkamona[2] (Awashonk's brother) and some others. Captain Church bade them go and prosper, and made Light-foot their chief, and gave him the title of captain. Bid them go and quit themselves like men. And away they scampered like so many horses. Next morning[3] early they returned to their Captain and informed him that they had come up with the enemy and killed several of them, and brought him thirteen of them prisoners; were mighty proud of their exploit, and rejoiced much at the opportunity of avenging themselves.

Captain Church sent the prisoners to Bridgwater and sent out his scouts to see what enemies or tracks they could. Discovering some small tracks, he follows them, found where the enemy had kindled some fires and roasted some flesh, but had put out their fires and were gone. The Captain followed them by the track, putting his Indians in the front; some of which were such as he had newly taken from the enemy and added to his company. Gave them order to march softly and, upon hearing a whistle in the rear, to sit down, till further order. Or, upon discovery of any enemy, to stop, for his design was, if he could discover where the enemy were, not to fall upon them (unless necessitated to do it) until next morning. The Indians in the front came up with many women and children and others that were faint and tired, and so not able to keep up with the company. These gave them an account that Philip, with a great number of the enemy, were a little before. Captain Church's Indians told the others they were their prisoners, but if they would submit to order and be still, no one should hurt them. They, being their old acquaintance, they were easily persuaded to conform.

A little before sunset there was a halt in the front until the Captain came up, and they told him they discovered the enemy. He ordered them to dog them and watch their motion till it was dark. But Philip soon came to a stop and fell to breaking and chopping wood to make fires; and a great noise they made. Captain Church draws his company up into a ring and sat down in the swamp without any noise or fire. The Indian prisoners were much surprised to see the English soldiers. But the Captain told them, if they would be quiet and not make any disturbances or noise, they should meet with civil treatment, but if they made any disturbance, or offered to run, or make their escape, he would immediately kill them all. So they were very submissive and obsequious.

When the day broke, Captain Church told his prisoners that his expedition was such at this time that he could not afford them any guard. Told them, they would find it to be their interest to attend the orders he was now about to give them, which was, that when the fight was over, which they now expected, or as soon as the firing ceased, they must follow the tracks of his company and come to them. (An Indian is next to a bloodhound to follow a track.) He said to them, it would be in vain for them to think of disobedience, or to gain anything by it, for he had taken and killed a great many of the Indian rebels and should in a little time kill and take all the rest.

By this time it began to be so light as the time that he usually chose to make his onset. He moved, sending two soldiers before to try if they could privately discover the enemy's postures. But very unhappily it fell out that the very same time Philip had sent two of his as a scout upon his own track, to see if none dogged them; who spied the two Indian men, and turned short about, and fled with all speed to their camp. And Captain Church pursued as fast as he could. The two Indians set a-yelling and howling, and made the most hideous noise they could invent; soon gave the alarm to Philip and his camp, who all fled at the first tidings, left their kettles boiling and meat roasting upon their wooden spits, and ran into a swamp, with no other breakfast than what Captain Church afterwards treated them with.

Philip's Forces Routed Near Bridgewater

Captain Church, pursuing, sent Mr. Isaac Howland,[1] with a party on one side of the swamp, while himself, with the rest, ran on the other side, agreeing to run on each side until they met on the further end, placing some men in secure stands at that end of the swamp where Philip entered, concluding that if they headed him and beat him back, that he would take back in his own track. Captain Church and Mr. Howland soon met at the further end of the swamp (it not being a great one), where they met with a great number of the enemy, well-armed, coming out of the swamp. But, on sight of the English, they seemed very much surprised and tacked short. Captain Church called hastily to them and said, if they fired one gun they were all dead men, for he would have them know that he had them hemmed in, with a force sufficient to command them; but if they peaceably surrendered, they should have good quarter.[2]

They, seeing both Indians and English come so thick upon them, were so surprised that many of them stood still and let the English come and take the guns out of their hands, when they were both charged and cocked. Many, both men, women, and children of the enemy were imprisoned at this time; while Philip, Tispaquin, Totoson, etc., concluded that the English would pursue them upon their tracks, so were waylaying their tracks at the first end of the swamp, hoping thereby to gain a shot upon Captain

Church, who was now better employed in taking his prisoners and running them into a valley, in form something shaped like a punch bowl, and, appointing a guard of two files triple-armed with guns taken from the enemy.

But Philip, having waited all this while in vain, now moves on after the rest of his company to see what was become of them. And, by this time, Captain Church was got into the swamp ready to meet him; and, as it happened, made the first discovery, clapped behind a tree until Philip's company came pretty near, and then fired upon them, killed many of them; and a close skirmish followed. Upon this, Philip, having grounds sufficient to suspect the event of his company that went before them, fled back upon his own track and, coming to the place where the ambush lay, they fired on each other, and one Lucas, of Plymouth, not being so careful as he might have been about his stand,[3] was killed by the Indians.

In this swamp skirmish, Captain Church with his two men which always ran by his side as his guard, met with three of the enemy, two of which surrendered themselves, and the Captain's guard seized them, but the other, being a great, stout, surly fellow, with his two locks tied up with red, and a great rattlesnake skin hanging to the back part of his head (whom Captain Church concluded to be Totoson), ran from them into the swamp. Captain Church, in person, pursued him close, till coming pretty near up with him, presented his gun between his shoulders, but, it missing fire, the Indian, perceiving it, turned and presented at Captain Church and, missing [missed] fire also, their guns taking wet with the fog and dew of the morning. But, the Indian, turning short for another run, his foot tripped in a small grapevine, and he fell flat on his face. Captain Church was by this time up with him and struck the muzzle of his gun an inch and half into the back part of his head, which dispatched him without another blow. But Captain Church, looking behind him, saw Totoson, the

Indian whom he thought he had killed, come flying at him like a dragon. But this happened to be fair in sight of the guard that were set to keep the prisoners, who, spying Totoson and others that were following of him, in the very seasonable juncture, made a shot upon them and rescued their Captain, though he was in no small danger from his friend's bullets, for some of them came so near him that he thought he felt the wind of them. The skirmish being over, they gathered their prisoners together and found the number that they had killed and taken was 173 (the prisoners which they took overnight included), who after the skirmish came to them, as they were ordered.[4]

Now, having no provisions but what they took from the enemy, they hastened to Bridgwater, sending an express before to provide for them, their company being now very numerous. The gentlemen of Bridgwater met Captain Church with great expression of honor and thanks, and received him and his army with all due respect and kind treatment.

Captain Church drove his prisoners that night into Bridgwater Pound, and set his Indian soldiers to guard them. They, being well treated with victuals and drink, they had a merry night; and the prisoners laughed as loud as the soldiers, not being so treated a long time before.

Some of the Indians now said to Captain Church, "Sir, you have now made Philip ready to die, for you have made him as poor and miserable as he used to make the English, for you have now killed or taken all his relations." That they believed he would now soon have his head, and that this bout had almost broke his heart.

The next day[5] Captain Church moved and arrived, with all his prisoners safe, at Plymouth. The great English army were now at Taunton, and Major Talcot, with the Connecticut forces being in these parts of the country, did considerable spoil upon the enemy.

Now Captain Church, being arrived at Plymouth, received thanks from the Government for his good service. Many of his soldiers were disbanded, and he thought to rest himself awhile, being much fatigued and his health impaired by excessive heats and colds and wading through rivers. But it was not long[6] before he was called upon to rally, upon advice that some of the enemy were discovered in Dartmouth woods. He took his Indians, and as many English volunteers as presented, to go with him. And, scattering into small parcels, Mr. Jabez Howland (who was now and often his lieutenant and a worthy good soldier) had the fortune to discover and imprison a parcel of the enemy.

In the evening they met together at an appointed place and, by examining the prisoners, they gained intelligence of Totoson's haunt; and, being brisk in the morning, they soon gained an advantage of Totoson's company, though he himself, with his son of about eight years old, made their escape, and one old squaw with them, to Agawom, his own country. But Sam Barrow,[7] as noted a rogue as any among the enemy, fell into the hands of the English at this time. Captain Church told him that because of his inhumane murders and barbarities, the Court had allowed him no quarter, but [he] was to be forthwith put to death, and, therefore, he was to prepare for it. Barrow replied that the sentence of death against him was just, and that indeed he was ashamed to live any longer, and desired no more favor than to smoke a whiff of tobacco before his execution. When he had taken a few whiffs, he said he was ready. Upon which, one of Captain Church's Indians sunk his hatchet into his brains.

Death of Totoson

The famous Totoson[1] arriving at Agawom, his son, which was the last which was left of his family (Captain Church having destroyed all the rest), fell sick. The wretch, reflecting upon the miserable condition he had brought himself into, his heart became as a stone within him, and he died. The old squaw flung a few leaves and a brush over him and came into Sandwich, and gave this account of his death, and offered to show them where she left his body; but never had the opportunity, for she immediately fell sick and died also.

Captain Church, being now at Plymouth again, weary and worn, would have gone home to his wife and family, but the Government being solicitous to engage him in the service until Philip was slain, and promising him satisfaction and redress for some mistreatment that he had met with, he fixes for another expedition. He had soon volunteers enough to make up the company he desired, and marched through the woods until he came to Pocasset.[2]

And not seeing nor hearing of any of the enemy, they went over the ferry to Rhode Island, to refresh themselves. The Captain, with about half-a-dozen in his company, took horse and rid about eight miles down the Island to Mr. Sanford's, where he had left his wife, who no sooner saw him but fainted with the surprise. And by that time she was a little revived, they spied two horsemen coming a great pace. Captain Church told his company that those men (by their riding) came with tidings.

When they came up, they proved to be Major Sanford and Captain Golding, who immediately asked Captain

Church what he would give to hear some news of Philip. He replied, that was what he wanted. They told him, they had rid hard with some hopes of overtaking him, and were now come on purpose to inform him that there was just now tidings from Mount-hope. An Indian came down from thence (where Philip's camp now was) on to Sand-point over against Trips,[3] and hallooed and made signs to be fetched over. And, being fetched over, he reported that he was fled from Philip, who (said he) has killed my brother just before I came away for giving some advice that displeased him. And said he was fled for fear of meeting with the same his brother had met with. Told them also that Philip was now in Mount-hope Neck.

Captain Church thanked them for their good news, and said, he hoped by tomorrow morning to have the rogue's head. The horses that he and his company came on standing at the door (for they had not been unsaddled), his wife must content herself with a short visit, when such game was ahead. They immediately mounted, set spurs to their horses, and away. The two gentlemen that brought him the tidings told him they would gladly wait upon him to see the event of this expedition.

He thanked them and told them he should be as fond of their company as any mens; and (in short) they went with him. And they were soon at Trip's Ferry (with Captain Church's company) where the deserter was; who was a fellow of good sense, and told his story handsomely. He offered Captain Church to pilot him to Philip and to help to kill him, that he might revenge his brother's death. Told him that Philip was now upon a little spot of upland that was in the south end of the mirey swamp just at the foot of the mount, which was a spot of ground that Captain Church was well acquainted with. By that time they were got over the ferry and came near the ground, half the night was spent. The Captain commands a halt and, bringing the company together, he asked Major Sanford and Captain

Golding's advice, what method was best to take in making the onset. But they declined giving any advice, telling him that his great experience and success forbid their taking upon them to give advice.

Philip Killed

Then Captain Church offered Captain Golding that he should have the honor (if he would please accept of it) to beat up Philip's headquarters. He accepted the offer and had his alloted number drawn out to him, and the pilot. Captain Church's instructions to him were to be very careful in his approach to the enemy, and be sure not to show himself until by daylight they might see and discern their own men from the enemy. Told him also that his custom in the like cases was to creep with his company on their bellies, until they came as near as they could; and that as soon as the enemy discovered them, they would cry out; and that was the word for his men to fire and fall on. Directed him, when the enemy should start and take into the swamp, they should pursue with speed, every man shouting and making what noise they could; for he would give orders to his ambuscade to fire on any that should come silently.

Captain Church, knowing it was Philip's custom to be foremost in flight, went down to the swamp and gave Captain William of Situate the command of the right wing of the ambush, and placed an Englishman and an Indian together behind such shelters of trees, that he could find and took care to place them at such distance as none might pass undiscovered between them; charged them to be careful of themselves and of hurting their friends; and to fire at any that should come silently through the swamp.

Death of Philip.

But it being somewhat further through the swamp than he was aware of, he wanted men to make up his ambuscade. Having placed what men he had, he took Major Sanford by the hand, said,

"Sir, I have so placed them that 'tis scarce possible Philip should escape them."

The same moment a shot whistled over their heads, and then the noise of a gun towards Philip's camp. Captain Church at first thought it might be some gun fired by accident, but, before he could speak, a whole volley followed, which was earlier than he expected. One of Philip's gang going forth to ease himself, when he had done, looked round him, and Captain Golding thought the Indian looked right at him (though probably 'twas but his conceit), so fired at him, and, upon his firing, the whole company that were with him fired upon the enemy's shelter before the Indians had time to rise from their sleep, and so overshot them. But their shelter was open on that side next the swamp, built so on purpose for the convenience of flight on occasion. They were soon in the swamp, and Philip the foremost, who, starting at the first gun, threw his petunk[1] and powder horn over his head, catched up his gun, and ran as fast as he could scamper, without any more clothes than his small breeches and stockings, and ran directly upon two of Captain Church's ambush. They let him come fair within shot, and the Englishman's[2] gun missing fire, he bid the Indian[3] fire away. And he did so to purpose, sent one musket bullet through his heart, and another not above two inches from it. He fell upon his face in the mud and water, with his gun under him.

By this time, the enemy perceived they were waylaid on the east side of the swamp, tacked short about. One of the enemy who seemed to be a great surly old fellow, hallooed with a loud voice and often called out, "Iootash! Iootash!"[4]

Captain Church called to his Indian, Peter,[5] and asked

him, who that was that called so? He answered, it was old Annawon, Philip's great captain, calling on his soldiers to stand to it and fight stoutly.

Lock of Gun that Killed Philip.

Now the enemy, finding that place of the swamp which was not ambushed, many of them made their escape in the English tracks. The man that had shot down Philip ran with all speed to Captain Church and informed him of his exploit, who commanded him to be silent about it and let no man more know it until they had drove the swamp clean. But, when they had drove the swamp through and found the enemy had escaped, or at least the most of them, and the sun now up, and so the dew gone, that they could not so easily track them, the whole company met together at the place where the enemies' night shelter was. And then Captain Church gave them the news of Philip's death upon which the whole army gave three loud huzzahs.

Captain Church ordered his body to be pulled out of the mire on to the upland, so some of Captain Church's Indians took hold of him by his stockings, and some, by his small breeches (being otherwise naked), and drew him through the mud unto the upland. And a doleful, great, naked, dirty beast he looked like.

Philip's Seat at Mount Hope.

Captain Church then said that, forasmuch as he had caused many an Englishman's body to lie unburied and rot above ground, that not one of his bones should be buried. And, calling his old Indian executioner bid him behead and quarter him.[6]

Accordingly, he came with his hatchet and stood over him, but, before he struck, he made a small speech, directing it to Philip, and said, he had been a very great man, and had made many a man afraid of him, but so big as he was, he would now chop his ass for him. And so went to work and did as he was ordered.

Philip, having one very remarkable hand, being much scarred, occasioned by the splitting of a pistol in it formerly, Captain Church gave the head and that hand to Alderman, the Indian who shot him, to show to such gentlemen as would bestow gratuities upon him. And accordingly, he got many a penny by it.

This being on the last day of the week,[7] the Captain with his company returned to the Island, tarried there until Tuesday; and then went off and ranged through all the woods to Plymouth, and received their premium, which was thirty shillings per head for all the enemies which they had killed or taken, instead of all wages. And Philip's head went at the same price. Methinks it's scanty reward and poor encouragement; though it was better than what had been some time before. For this march they received four shillings and sixpence a man, which was all the reward they had, except the honor of killing Philip. This was in the latter end of August, 1676.

The Cold Spring Monument at Mount Hope.

The Search for Annawon

Captain Church had been but a little while at Plymouth, before a post from Rehoboth came to inform the Government that old Annawon, Philip's chief captain was with his company ranging about their woods and was very offensive and pernicious to Rehoboth and Swansey. Captain Church was immediately sent for again and treated with to engage one expedition more. He told them, their encouragement was so poor, he feared his soldiers would be dull about going again. But, being a hearty friend to the cause, he rallies again, goes to Mr. Jabesh Howland, his old lieutenant, and some of his soldiers that used to go out with him, told them how the case was circumstanced, and that he had intelligence of old Annawon's walk and haunt, and wanted hands to hunt him. They did not want much entreating, but told him, they would go with him as long as there was an Indian left in the woods.

He moved,[1] and ranged through the woods to Pocasset. It, being the latter end of the week, he proposed to go on to Rhode Island and rest until Monday. But, early on the Lord's Day morning, there came a post to inform the Captain that early the same morning a canoe with several Indians in it passed from Prudence Island to Poppasquash Neck.[2] Captain Church thought, if he would possibly surprise them, he might probably gain some intelligence of more game. Therefore, he made all possible speed after them.

The ferry boat being out of the way, he made use of canoes. But, by that time they had made two freights, and got over the Captain and about 15 or 16 of his Indians, the wind sprung up with such violence that canoes could no more pass. The Captain, seeing it was impossible for any more of his soldiers to come to him, he told his Indians, if they were willing to go with him, he would go to Poppasquash and see if they could catch some of those enemy Indians. They were willing to go, but were sorry they had no English soldiers. So they marched through the thickets, that they might not be discovered, until they came unto the salt meadow to the northward of Bristol Town, that now is.

Then they heard a gun. The Captain looked about, not knowing but it might be some of his own company in the rear. So, halting till they all came up, he found 'twas none of his own company that fired. Now, though he had but a few men, was minded to send some of them out on a scout. He moved it to Captian Lightfoot to go with three more on a scout. He said he was willing, provided the Captain's man, Nathanael (which was an Indian that they had lately taken), might be one of them, because he was well acquainted with the neck, and, coming lately from among them, knew how to call[3] them.

The Captain bid him choose his three companions and go; and, if they came across any of the enemy, not to kill them if they could possibly take them alive; that they might gain intelligence concerning Annawon. The Captain with the rest of his company moved but a little way further toward Poppasquash before they heard another gun, which seemed to be the same way with the other, but further off.

But they made no halt until they came unto the narrow of Poppasquash Neck, where Captain Church left three men more, to watch if any should come out of the neck, and to inform the scout when they returned which way he was gone. He parted the remainder of his company, half on one side of the neck, and the other with himself went on the other side of the neck, until they met; and, meeting neither with Indians nor canoes, returned big with expectations of tidings by their scout. But when they came back to the three men at the narrow of the neck, they told their Captain the scout was not returned, had heard nor seen anything of them. This filled them with thoughts what should become of them. By that time they had sat down and waited an hour longer, it was very dark, and they despaired of their returning to them.

Some of the Indians told their Captain, they feared his new man Nathanael had met with his old Mount-hope friends and was turned rogue.

They concluded to make no fires that night (and indeed they had no great need of any), for they had no victuals to cook and had not so much as a morsel of bread with them. They took up their lodging, scattering, that if possibly their scout should come in the night, and whistle (which was their sign), some or other of them might hear them.

They had a very solitary, hungry night; and as soon as the day broke,[4] they drew off through the brush to a hill without the neck and, looking about them, they espied one

Indian man come running somewhat towards them. The Captain ordered one man to step out of the brush and show himself. Upon which the Indian ran right to him, and who should it be but Captain Lightfoot, to their great joy.

Captain Church asked him, "What news?"

He answered, Good News; they were all well and had catched ten Indians, and that they guarded them all night in one of the flankers of the old English garrison;[5] that their prisoners were part of Annawon's company, and that they had left their families in a swamp above Mattapoiset Neck.

And as they were marching toward the old garrison, Lightfoot gave Captain Church a particular account of their exploit, viz., that presently after they left him, they heard another gun, which seemed to be towards the Indian burying-place, and, moving that way, they discovered two of the enemy flaying an horse. The scout, clapping into the brush, Nathanael bid them sit down, and he would presently call all the Indians thereabout unto him. They hid; and he went a little distance back from them and sat up his note and howled like a wolf. One of the two immediately left his horse and came running to see who was there. But Nathanael, howling lower and lower, drew him in between those that lay in wait for him, who seized him. Nathanael continuing the same note, the other left the horse also, following his mate, and met with the same.

When they caught these two, they examined them apart, and found them to agree in their story, that there were eight more of them come down into the neck to get provisions, and had agreed to meet at the burying-place that evening. These two being some of Nathanael's old acquaintance, he had great influence upon them, and with his enticing story (telling what a brave Captain he had, how bravely he lived since he had been with him, and how much they might better their condition by turning to him, persuaded and engaged them to be on his side, which indeed now began to be the better side of the hedge. They waited but a little while before they espied the rest of theirs coming up to the burying-place, and Nathanael soon howled them in as he had done their mates before.

When Captain Church came to the garrison, he met his lieutenant and the rest of his company; and then, making up good fires, they fell to roasting their horse-beef, enough to last them the whole day, but had not a morsel of bread; though salt they had which they always carried in their pockets, which, at this time, was very acceptable to them.

Their next motion was towards the place where the prisoners told them they had left their women and children, and surprised them all, and some others that were newly come to them. And, upon examination, they held to one story, that it was hard to tell where to find Annawon, for he never roosted twice in a place.

Now a certain Indian soldier, that Captain Church had gained over to be on his side, prayed that he might have liberty to go and fetch in his father, who he said was about four miles from that place, in a swamp with no other than one young squaw. Captain Church inclined to go with him, thinking it might be in his way to gain some intelligence of Annawon. And so, taking one Englishman and a few Indians with him, leaving the rest there, he went with his new soldier to look [for] his father.

When he came to the swamp, he bid the Indian go see if he could find his father. He was no sooner gone, but Captain Church discovered a track coming down out of the woods, upon which he and his little company lay close, some on one side of the track and some on the other. They heard the Indian soldier make a howling for his father; and at length, somebody answered him. But while they were listening, they thought they heard somebody coming towards them, presently saw an old man coming up with a gun on his shoulder, and a young woman following of him in the track which they lay by. They let them come up between them, and then started up and laid hold on them both.

The Capture of Annawon

Captain Church immediately examined them apart, telling them what they must trust to if they told false stories. He asked the young woman, what company they came last from? She said, from Captain Annawon's. He asked her, how many were in company with him when she left him. She said, 50 or 60. He asked her, how many miles it was to the place where she left him? She said, she did not understand miles, but he was up in Squannaconk Swamp.[1]

The old man, who had been one of Philip's Council, upon examination, gave exactly the same account. Captain Church asked him, if they could get there that night? He said, if they went presently and travelled stoutly, they might get there by sunset. He asked, whither he was going? He answered, that Annawon had sent him down to look for some Indians that were gone into Mount-hope Neck to kill provisions. Captain Church let him know that those Indians were all his prisoners.

By this time came the Indian soldier and brought his father and one Indian more. The Captain was now in great straight of mind what to do next. He had a mind to give Annawon a visit, now knew where to find him, but his company was very small, but half-a-dozen men beside himself, and was under a necessity to send somebody back to acquaint his lieutenant and company with his proceedings. However, he asked his small company that were with him, whether they would willingly go with him and give Annawon a visit? They told him, they were always ready to obey his commands. But withal told him, that they knew this Captain Annawon was a great soldier, that he had been a valiant captain under Asuhmequn,[2] Philip's father; and that he had been Philip's chieftain all this war, a very subtle man and of great resolution, and had often said that he would never be taken alive by the English. And, moreover, they knew that the men that were with him were resolute fellows, some of Philip's chief soldiers, and therefore feared whether it was practicable to make an attempt upon him with so small a handful of assistants as now were with him. Told him further, that it would be a pity that, after all the great things he had done, he should throw away his life at last.

Upon which he replied, that he doubted not Annawon was a subtle and valiant man, that he had a long time but in vain sought for him, and never till now could find his quarters; and he was very loath to miss of the opportunity and doubted not but that if they would cheerfully go with him, the same Almighty Providence that had hitherto protected and befriended them would do so still.

Upon this, with one consent, they said they would go.

Captain Church then turned to one Cook,[3] of Plymouth (the only Englishman then with him), and asked him, what he thought if it? Who replied, "Sir, I am never afraid of going anywhere when you are with me."

Then Captain Church asked the old Indian if he could carry his horse with him? (for he conveyed a horse thus far with him).

He replied that it was impossible for an horse to pass the swamps. Therefore, he sent away his new Indian soldier with his father and the Captain's horse to his lieutenant and orders for him to move to Taunton with the prisoners, to secure them there, and to come out in the morning in the Rehoboth Road, in which he might expect to meet him, if he were alive and had success.

The Captain then asked the old fellow, if he would

pilot him unto Annawon? He answered that he, having given him his life, he was obliged to serve him. He bid him move on then; and they followed. The old man would out-travel them, so far sometimes that they were almost out of sight. Looking over his shoulder and seeing them behind, he would halt. Just as the sun was setting, the old man made a full stop and sat down, the company coming up also sat down, being all weary.

Massasoit's Pipe.

Philip's "Samp" or Porridge Bowl.

Niantic Mortar and Pestle.

Captain Church asked, "What news?"

He answered that about that time in the evening Captain Annawon sent out his scouts to see if the coast were clear, and, as soon as it began to grow dark, the scouts return. And then (said he), we may move again securely.

When it began to grow dark, the old man stood up again. Captain Church asked him if he would take a gun and fight for him? He bowed very low and prayed him not to impose such a thing upon him, as to fight against Captain Annawon, his old friend. "But," says he, "I will go along with you, and be helpful to you, and will lay hands on any man that shall offer to hurt you."

It being now pretty dark, they moved close together. Anon, they heard a noise; the Captain stayed the old man with his hand and asked his own men what noise they thought it might be? They concluded it to be the pounding of a mortar. The old man had given Captain Church a description of the place where Annawon now lay, and of the difficulty of getting at him. Being sensible that they were pretty near them, with two of his Indians he creeps to the edge of the rocks, from whence he could see their camps.[4]

He saw three companies of Indians at a little distance from each other, being easy to be discovered by the light of their fires. He saw also the great Annawon and his company, who had formed his camp or kennelling-place by felling a tree under the side of the great clefts of rocks, and setting a row of birch bushes up against it, where he himself and his son and some of his chiefs had taken up their lodging, and made great fires without them, and had their pots and kettles boiling and spits roasting. Their arms also he discovered, all set together in a place fitted for the purpose, standing up on end against a stick lodged in two crotches, and a mat placed over them, to keep them from the wet or dew. The old Annawon's feet and his son's head were so near the arms as almost to touch them. But the rocks were so steep that it was impossible to get down but as they lowered themselves by the boughs and the bushes that grew in the cracks of the rock.

Captain Church, creeping back again to the old man, asked him if there was no possibility of getting at them some other way. He answered, no, that he and all that belonged to Annawon were ordered to come that way, and none could come any other way without difficulty or danger of being shot.

Captain Church then ordered the old man and his daughter to go down foremost, with their baskets at their backs, so that, when Annawon saw them with their baskets, he should not mistrust the intrigue. Captain Church and his handful of soldiers crept down also under the shadow of these two and their baskets, and the Captain himself crept close behind the old man, with his hatchet in his hand, and stepped over the young man's head to the arms. The young Annawon, discovering of him, whipped his blanket over his head and shrunk up in a heap. The old Captain Annawon started up on his breech and cried out "Howoh!"[5] and, despairing of escape, threw himself back again, and lay silent until Captain Church had secured all the arms.

And, having secured that company, he sent his Indian soldiers to the other fires and companies, giving them instructions what to do and say. Accordingly, they went into the midst of them. When they discovered themselves who they were, told them that their Captain Annawon was taken, and it would be best for them quietly and peaceably to surrender themselves, which would procure good quarter for them. Otherwise, if they should pretend to resist or make their escape, it would be in vain, and they could expect no other but that Captain Church with his great army, who had now entrapped them, would cut them to pieces. Told them also if they would submit themselves, and deliver up all their arms unto them, and keep every man his place until it was day, they would assure them that their Captain Church who had been so kind to themselves when they surrendered to him, should be as kind unto them.

Now, they being old acquaintance, and many of them relations, did much the readier give heed to what they said, and complied and surrendered up their arms unto them, both their guns and hatchets, and were forthwith carried to Captain Church.

Things being so far settled, Captain Church asked Annawon what he had for supper, for (said he), "I am come to sup with you."

"Taubut,"[6] said Annawon, with a big voice; and, looking about upon his women, bid them hasten and get Captain Church and his company some supper; then turned to Captain Church and asked him whether he would eat cow-beef or horse-beef. The Captain told him cow-beef would be most acceptable. It was soon got ready, and, pulling his little bag of salt out of his pocket, which was all the provision he brought with him, this seasoned his cow-beef so that with it and the dried green corn, which the old squaw was pounding in the mortar, while they were sliding down the rocks, he made a very hearty supper. And this pounding in the mortar proved lucky for Captain Church's getting down the rocks, for when the old squaw pounded, they moved, and when she ceased to turn the corn, they ceased creeping. The noise of the mortar prevented the enemies' hearing their creeping; and the corn being now dressed, supplied the want of bread and gave a fine relish with the cow-beef.

Supper being over, Captain Church sent two of his men to inform the other companies that he had killed Philip, and had taken their friends in Mount-hope Neck, but had spared their lives, and that he had subdued now all the enemy (he supposed) excepting this company of Annawon's, and now, if they would be orderly and keep their places until morning, they should have good quarter, and that he would carry them to Taunton, where they might see their friends again. The messengers returned that the Indians yielded to his proposals.

Captain Church thought it was now time for him to take a nap, having had no sleep in two days and one night before. Told his men that, if they would let him sleep two hours, they should sleep all the rest of the night. He laid himself down and endeavored to sleep, but all disposition to sleep departed from him. After he had lain a little while, he looked up to see how his watch managed, but found them all fast asleep.

Now, Captain Church had told Captain Annawon's company, as he had ordered his Indians to tell the others, that their lives should all be spared, excepting Captain Annawon's, and it was not in his power to promise him his life, but he must carry him to his masters at Plymouth, and he would entreat them for his life.

Now, when Captain Church found not only his own men, but all the Indians fast asleep, Annawon only excepted, whom he perceived was as broad awake as himself; and so they lay looking one upon the other perhaps an hour. Captain Church said nothing to him, for he could not speak Indian, and thought Annawon could not speak English. At length, Annawon raised himself up, cast off his blanket, and with no more clothes than his small breeches, walked a little way back from the company. Captain Church thought no other but that he had occasion to ease himself, and so walked to some distance rather than offend him with the stink. But, by and by, he was gone out of sight and hearing; and then Captain Church began to suspect some ill-design in him, and got all the guns close to him, and crowded himself close under young Annawon, that if he should anywhere get a gun, he should not make a shot at him without endangering his son. Lying very still awhile, waiting for the event, at length he heard somebody coming the same way that Annawon went. The moon now shining bright, he saw him at a distance coming with something in his hands, and, coming up to Captain Church, he fell upon his knees before him and offered him what he had brought. And, speaking in plain English, said,

"Great Captain, you have killed Philip and conquered his country, for I believe that I and my company are the last that war against the English, so suppose the war is ended by your means; and therefore these things belong unto you."

Philip's Regalia

Then, opening his pack, he pulled out Philip's belt, curiously wrought with wompom, being nine inches broad, wrought with black and white wompom in various figures and flowers, and pictures of many birds and beasts. This, when hung upon Captain Church's shoulders, it reached his ankles. And another belt of wompom he presented him with, wrought after the former manner, which Philip was wont to put upon his head. It had two flags on the back part which hung down on his back, and another small belt with a star upon the end of it, which he used to hang on his breast. And they were all edged with red hair, which Annawon said they got in the Muh-hog's[1] country. Then he pulled out two horns of glazed powder and a red cloth blanket. He told Captain Church, these were Philip's royalties which he was wont to adorn himself with when he sat in state. That he thought himself happy that he had an opportunity to present them to Captain Church, who had won them.[2] Spent the remainder of the night in discourse, and gave an account of what mighty success he had formerly in wars against many nations of Indians, when served Asuhmequin, Philip's father.

In the morning as soon as it was light, the Captain marched with his prisoners out of that swampy country towards Taunton, met his lieutenant and company about four miles out of town, who expressed a great deal of joy to see him again and said 'twas more than ever he expected. They went into Taunton, were civilly and kindly treated by the inhabitants, refreshed and rested themselves that night.

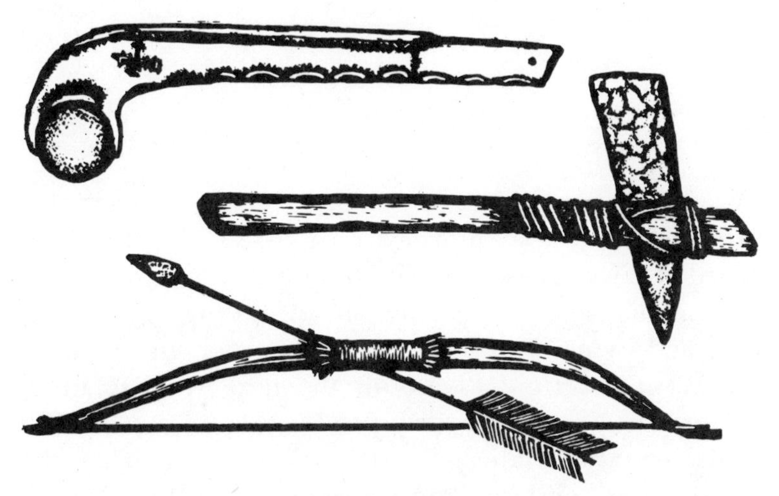

Indian Weapons.

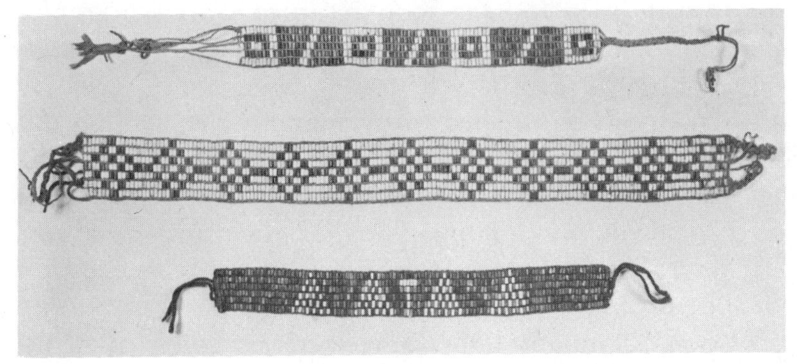

Wampum.

Early next morning, the Captain took old Annawon, and half-a-dozen Indian soldiers, and his own man, and went to Rhode Island, sending the rest of his company and his prisoners by his lieutenant to Plymouth. Tarrying two or three days upon the Island, he then went to Plymouth, and carried his wife and his two children with him.

Tuspaquin, Last of Philip's Captains

Captain Church had been but a little while at Plymouth, before he was informed of a parcel of Indians that haunted the woods between Plymouth and Sippican, that did great damage to the English in killing their cattle, horses, and swine. And the Captain was soon in pursuit of them. Went out from Plymouth the next Monday in the afternoon. Next·morning early they discovered a track. The Captain sent two Indians on the track to see what they could discover, while he and his company followed gently after, but the two Indians soon returned with tidings that they had discovered the enemy sitting round their fires, in a thick place of brush. When they came pretty near the place, the Captain ordered every man to creep as he did, and surround them by creeping as near as they could, till they should be discovered, and then to run on upon them and take them alive, if possible (for their prisoners were their pay). They did so; took every one that was at the fires, not one escaping.

Upon examination, they agreed in their story, that they belonged to Tispaquin, who was gone with John Bump, and one more, to Agawom and Sippican to kill horses, and were not expected back in two or three days. This same Tispaquin had been a great captain, and there Indians reported that he was such a great Pouwau[1] that no bullet could enter him.

Captain Church said he would not have him killed, for there was a war broke out in the eastern part of the country, and he would have him saved to go with them to fight the eastern Indians. Agreeably, he left two old squaws of the prisoners, and bid them tarry until their Captain Tispaquin returned, and to tell him that Church had been there, and had taken his wife, children, and company, and carried them down to Plymouth. And would spare all their lives, and his too, if he would come down to them and bring the other two that were with him, and they should be his soldiers.

Captain Church then returned to Plymouth, leaving the old squaws well provided for, and biscuit for Tispaquin when he returned. Telling his soldiers that he doubted not but he had laid a trap that would take him.

Captain Church, two days after, went to Boston (the Commissioners then sitting), and waited upon the Honorable Governor Leverett, who then lay sick, who requested of Captain Church to give him some account of the war. Who readily obliged His Honor therein, to his great satisfaction, as he was pleased to express himself, taking him by the hand, and telling him, if it pleased God he lived, he would make it a brace of a hundred pounds' advantage to him out of the Massachusetts Colony, and would endeavor the rest of the colonies should do proportionably. But he died within a fortnight after,[2] and so nothing was done of that nature.

The same day Tispaquin came in, and those that were with him, but when Captain Church returned from Boston, he found to his grief that the heads of Annawon, Tispaquin, [had been] cut off, which were the last of Philip's friend's. The General Court[3] of Plymouth, then sitting, sent for Captain Church, who waited upon them accordingly, and received their thanks for his good service, which they unanimously voted, which was all that Captain Church had for his aforesaid service.

Afterwards in the year 1676[4] in the month of January, Captain Church received a Commission from Governor Winslow, to scour the woods of some of the lurking enemy, which they were well informed were there. Which Commission is as follows:

BEing well informed that there are certain parties of our Indian *Enemies, (remains of the People, or Allies of* Philip, *late Sachem of* Mount-hope, *our Mortal Enemy) that are still lurking in the Woods near some of our Plantations, that go on to disturb the Peace of His Majesty's Subjects in this & the Neighbouring Colonies, by their frequent Robberies, and other Insolences. Captain* Benjamin Church *is therefore hereby Nominated, Ordered, Commissioned, and Impowred to raise a Company of Volunteers, consisting of* English *and* Indians; *so many as he shall judge necessary to improve in the present Expedition, and can obtain; And of them to take the Command, and Conduct, and to lead them forth unto such place or places within this or the Neighbouring Colonies, as he shall think fit, and as the Providence of God, and his Intelligence may lead him; To Discover, Pursue, Fight, Surprize, Destroy, and Subdue our said* Indian *Enemy, or any party or parties of them, that by the Providence of God they may meet with; Or them, or any of them to receive to Mercy, if he see cause (provided they be not Murderous Rogues, or such as have been principal Actors in those Vilanies.) And for the Prosecution of the design, liberty is hereby granted to the said Capt.* Church, *and others to Arm and set out such of our friendly* Indians, *as he is willing to Entertain. And forasmuch as all our Enemies that have been taken, or at*

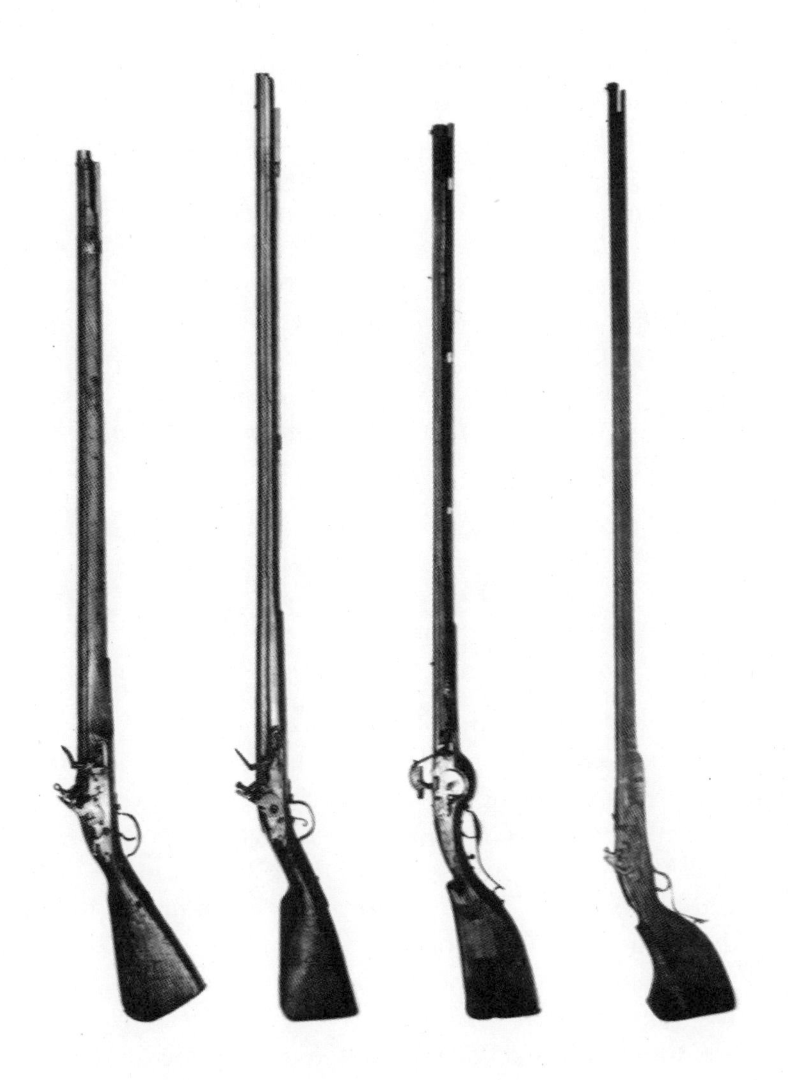

Flintlocks of the Seventeenth Century.

any time may be taken by our Forces, have by our Courts and Councils been rendred lawful Captives of War, and condemned to perpetual Servitude; this Council do also determine and hereby declare, That all such Prisoners as by the blessing of God the said Captain and Company, or any of them, shall take, together with their Arms, and other Plunder, shall be their own, and to be distributed amongst themselves, according to such agreement as they may be at one with another: And it shall be lawful, and is hereby warrantable for him and them to make Sale of such Prisoners as their perpetual Slaves; or otherwise to retain and keep them as they think meet, (they being such as the Law allows to be kept:) Finally, the said Capt. Church *herein improving his best judgment and discretion, and utmost ability, faithfully to Serve the Interest of God, his Majesties Interest, and the Interest of the Colony; and carefully governing his said Company at home and abroad; these shall be unto him full and ample Commission, Warrant and Discharge. Given under the Publick Seal.* January 15th. 1676

Per Josiah Winslow, GOV.

Accordingly, Captain Church, accompanied with several gentlemen and others went out and took divers parties of Indians. And in one of which parties there was a certain old man whom Captain Church seemed to take particular notice of and, asking him where he belonged, who told him, to Swanzey; the Captain asked his name, who replied his name was Conscience.

"Conscience," said the Captain (smiling), "then the war is over, for that was what they were searching for, it being much wanted." And then returned the said Conscience to his post again at Swanzey, to a certain person the said Indian desired to be sold to, and returned home.

Tombstones of Benjamin Church and His Wife Alice, Little Compton.

Lydia Tuspaquin, Eighth Descendant of Massasoit.

Appendix I

The Mythical History of King Philip

Historical figures like King Philip—powerful, impenetrable, tragic, symbolic—generate myths.

At the simplest of all levels there is the myth which links material objects to the great name. England used to be full of inns and houses where Mary Queen of Scots was said to have slept. Samuel Drake once asked a Providence auctioneer—this was nearly a century and a half ago—whether he had ever sold an oil painting of Roger Williams, and was told he did not think he had, but that he had sold many guns that belonged to King Philip and enough furniture that came over with the Mayflower to freight a first-class man-of-war.[1] So we have Philip's pipe in the Museum of the American Indian,[2] Philip's bead belt in the Museum of the Rhode Island Historical Society,[3] Philip's samp bowl in the Peabody Museum,[4] Philip's Lookout at Assawompsett, Philip's Seat on Mount Hope. When some incised banner-stones showed up at Warren, it was inevitably suggested that members of King Philip's tribe must have produced them.[5] These are the myths for the children's hour.

More sophisticated are the myths of the historians and the historical romances. As we study the characterizations of King Philip over the last three centuries we feel as if we are meeting in turn Philip the Bad, Philip the Great, Philip the Good, Philip the Feeble. When the evidence about his feelings, thoughts and capacities is as meager as it is, there is all the more room for invention.

Finally, there are the myths involved in the effort of one culture to interpret another. Though these are obvious enough at the level of verbal interpretation, they are most striking in the visual arts. Imagine the feelings of a modern Indian, attuned by the discoveries of "black studies" to the possibilities of "red studies," as he looks at the white man's efforts to portray the Indians of New England—the opulent, Frenchified curves of Champlain's Indians, the puny Ninigret, the pimply, morose Philip in Revere's engraving, the Byronic whims of Drake's engraver, the brooding, bloodless Philips of the mid-nineteenth-century illustrators, the enamelled, barbered Philip of 1892 in the Kennedy Galleries.[6] What a racist mish-mash of cartoonery, buffoonery and sentimentalism! We can hear the Indian saying, "The white man can only paint the white man!"

Perhaps the closest we can get to the Algonquian Indian of the seventeenth century is through a photograph of one of his descendants. It is not very close, given the inevitable changes in blood and sensibility. But are we, too, romancing when we find in a Lydia Tuspaquin or an Emma Stafford the sinewy strength and solidity which Church must have found in Philip?[7]

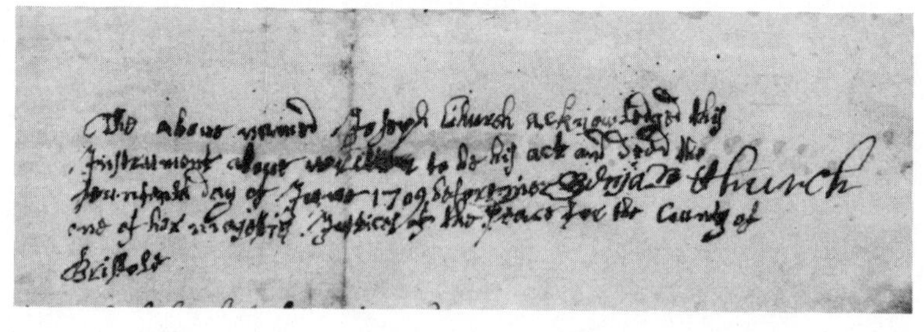
The above named Joseph Church acknowledged this instrument above written to be his act and deed this fourteenth day of June 1709 before me Benja Church one of her majesty's Justices of the Peace for the County of Bristol

Autographs of Benjamin and Joseph Church.

Appendix II

Previous Editions of Benjamin Church's Narrative

First Edition (1716)

Entertaining Passages relating to Philip's War which Began in the Month of June 1675. As also of Expeditions More Lately Made against the Common Enemy and Indian Rebels, in the Eastern Parts of New-England: with Some Account of the Divine Providence towards Benj. Church Esqr. By T.C. Boston: Printed by B. Green, in the Year 1716. 4to. Pp. 2+120. 19cm.

Second Edition (1772)

The Entertaining History of King Philip's War, which Began in the Month of June, 1675. As also of Expeditions More Lately Made against the Common Enemy and Indian Rebels in the Eastern Parts of New-England, with Some Account of the Divine Providence towards Col. Benjamin Church: By Thomas Church, Esq., His Son. The Second Edition. Boston: Printed, 1716. Newport, Rhode-Island: Reprinted and Sold by Solomon Southwick, in Queen-Street, 1772. 8vo. Pp. iv + 5—198 + (1). 2 portraits incl. frontispiece (King Philip and Church, fictitious, engravings by Paul Revere). 18½ cm.

Drake's Two Editions (1825, 1827)*

The History of King Philip's War; also of Expeditions against the French and Indians in the Eastern Parts of New-England, in the years 1689, 1690, 1692, 1696 and 1704. With Some Account of the Divine Providence towards Col. Benjamin Church. By His Son, Thomas Church, Esq. To Which is Now Added, an Index, Copious Notes and Corrections. Also, an Appendix, containing a Sketch of the Discovery of America, Landing of the Pilgrims at Plymouth, together with the Most Important Indian Wars to the Time of the Creek War. By Samuel G. Drake. Boston: Howe & Norton, Printers, 1825. 12mo. Pp. xiv + [15]-304. Frontispiece (Portrait of King Philip). 18½ cm.

The History of King Philip's War, Commonly Called the Great Indian War, of 1675 and 1676. Also of the French and Indians Wars at the Eastward, in 1689, 1690, 1692, 1696, and 1704. By Thomas Church, Esq. With Numerous Notes to Explain the Situation of the Places of Battles, the Particular Geography of the Ravaged Country, and the Lives of the Principal Persons Engaged in Those Wars. Also, an Appendix, Containing an Account of the Treatment of the Natives by the Early Voyagers, the Settlement of N. England by the Forefathers, the Pequot War, Narratives of Persons Carried into Captivity, Anecdotes of the Indians, and the Most Important Indian Wars to the Time of the Creek War. By Samuel G. Drake. Second Edition, with Plates. Boston: Printed by J.H.A. Frost [1827]. Pp. xvi + [17]-360. 2 plates; 2 portraits. 18½ cm.

Reissues of Drake's 1827 Edition From Stereotype Plates

1. Boston: J.H.A. Frost, 1827. This edition, the first one from stereotype plates (an early example of their use) duplicates the edition printed by Frost in 1827 except that it lacks the initial "The" at beginning of the Title. 2 plates; 2 portraits.

2. Boston: T. B. Wait & son, 1827. 12 mo. 2 plates; 2 portraits.

3. Exeter, N. H.: J. & B. Williams, 1829. Frontispiece (Landing of the Pilgrims). 12 mo.

4. Boston: M. Mower & Co., 1829. 16 mo. 2 plates; 2 portraits.

5. Exeter, N. H.: J. & B. Williams, 1834. 16 mo. Frontispiece (Landing of the Pilgrims).

6. Exeter, N. H.: J. & B. Williams, 1836. 16 mo. Frontispiece (Landing of the Pilgrims).

7. Exeter, N. H.: J. & B. Williams, 1839.

8. Exeter, N. H.: J. & B. Williams, 1840. 16 mo. 1 plate.

9. Exeter, N. H.: J. & B. Williams, 1842. 16 mo. 1 plate. (Capture of Annawon).

10. Exeter, N. H.: J. & B. Williams, 1843. 16 mo. 1 plate (Capture of Annawon).

11. *The History of the Great Indian War of 1675 and 1676, Commonly Called Philip's War. Also, the Old French and Indian Wars from 1689 to 1704* By Thomas Church,

Esq. With numerous Notes and an Appendix, by Samuel G. Drake. Revised Edition. Hartford: S. Andrus & Son [1845]. 8 vo. With plates.

12. N. Y.: H. Dayton [1845] 8 vo. 7 plates; 5 portraits.

13. Cooperstown [N. Y.]: H. & E. Phinney, 1846. 12 mo. 1 portrait; 3 plates. Plates are inferior new woodcuts on yellow paper.

14. Cooperstown: H. & E. Phinney, 1848. 12 mo. Frontispiece. Portrait.

15. Hartford: S. Andrus & Son, 1851. 12 mo. No illustrations. 19½ cm.

16. Hartford: S. Andrus & Son, 1852. 12 mo. 19½ cm.

17. Hartford: S. Andrus & Son, 1854. 24 cm.

18. Hartford: S. Andrus & Son, [1855].

19. New York: H. Dayton, 1859. 8 vo.

20. New York: H. Dayton, 1860. 8 vo. 23½ cm. Without illustrations.

21. Boston: J. H. A. Frost, 1887.

22. Boston: J. H. A. Frost, 1889.

Church's "Entertaining Episodes" also appeared in S. L. Knapp's *Library of American History* (N. Y.: Leavitt and Allen, 1836-37), Vol. II, 236-77. The "Library" was published originally in weekly numbers under the title "The American Library." A Centennial Edition of this work, entitled *The People's History of America . . .* was published in 1876 by H. S. Allen in New York. 4 to. Church is reprinted on pp. 681-720. Another reprint appeared in *The Two Americas,* (New York, 1879), pp. 681-720 And in the 1881 edition of the same work.

Dexter's Edition (1865)

The History of King Philip's War. By Benjamin Church. With an Introduction and Notes by Henry Martyn Dexter. Boston: John Kimball Wiggin, 1865. 4to. Pp. 205. ("Library of N. E. History," No. 2.) 250 copies only in fcap 4to. and 35 on large paper, rl 4to.

*Note: In his Preface to *The Book of the Indians* 9th ed. Boston, 1848, Drake wrote:

"My first publication upon the subject of the Indians was an edition of Church's History of Philip's War, a duodecimo with notes and appendix. This was in the summer of 1825; and in 1827, it was considerably enlarged, and issued in a second edition, the copyright of which, not long after, passed out of my hands, and the number of editions since issued is unkown to me; but about two years since, one of the proprietors told me they amounted to some thirty or forty; yet 'second edition' is continued in the title-page to this day.[1848]"

Appendix III

Suggestions for Reading

1. SEVENTEENTH CENTURY SOURCES

(a) Background Reading

Classic descriptions of Colonial life and of Indian life in New England before King Philip's War may be sampled in the following works:

Bradford, William. *Of Plymouth Plantation, 1620-1647.* Edited by S. E. Morison. New York, 1952.

Gardiner, Lion. *A History of the Pequot War . . .left in Manuscript by Lieutenant Lion Gardiner, an Actor in That War Who Resided in the Midst of Those Indians.* Cincinnati, 1800.

Gookin, Daniel. *Historical Collections of the Indians in New England; of Their Several Nations, Numbers, Customs, Manners, Religion and Government before the English Planted there.* Boston, 1792. Edited by Jeffrey H. Fiske, Towtaid, 1970.

Higginson, Francis. *New Englands Plantation; or a Short and True Description of the Commodities and Discommodities of that Country.* London, 1630. Reprinted, Essex Book and Print Club, Salem, Mass., 1908.

Josselyn, John. "An Account of Two Voyages to New England, 1674," *Mass. Hist. Soc. Coll.,* 3 ser., III (1833), pp. 211-354.

—— *New Englands Rarities Discovered: in Birds, Beasts, Fishes, Serpents, and Plants of That Country.* London,

1672. Reprinted, in facsimile, Boston: Massachusetts Historical Society, 1972.

Morton, Nathaniel. *New England's Memorial.* Boston, 1669. Reprinted Newport, 1772, Plymouth 1826, Boston 1903, New York 1937.

—— "The New English Canaan." Edited by Charles Francis Adams, Jr. in *Publications of the Prince Society,* XIV, Boston, 1883. Also in *Old South Leaflets,* Vol. IV, No. 87.

Mourt's Relation. The Journal of the Pilgrims at Plymouth, in New England, in 1620. London, 1622. Republished New York, 1848 (ed. by George B. Cheever) and 1963 (ed. by Dwight B. Heath) and Ann Arbor, Michigan ("March of America Facsimile Series," No. 21), 1966.

Orr, Charles (ed.). *History of the Pequot War; The Contemporary Accounts of Mason, Underhill, Vincent and Gardener.* Reprinted from the Mass. Hist. Soc. Coll. Cleveland, 1897.

Williams, Roger. *A Key into the Language of America.* London 1643. Republished in the *Publications of the Narragansett Club,* I, Providence 1866, and by the Wayne State University Press, 1973.

Winslow, Edward, "Good Newes from New England," London, 1624. Reprinted in Edward Arber, (ed.), *The Story of the Pilgrim Fathers* (London, 1897), pp. 509-600. Also New York, Kraus Reprint Co., 1969.

[Winthrop, John]. Hosmer, J.K., (ed): Winthrop's Journal "History of New England 1630-1649." 2 Vols. *Original Narratives of Early American History.* New York, 1908.

(b) Contemporary Accounts of the War.

Narratives and newsletters were written during the war for the benefit of readers in New England and Old England. Some of these, such as William Hubbard's and Increase

Mather's, were published in Boston and London in 1676 and 1677. Others, such as William Harris's letters to members of the English government, were only published in the twentieth century. Samuel Gardner Drake reprinted everything he could find between 1836 and 1867. Other reprints appeared in *Old South Leaflets* and Charles H. Lincoln's *Narratives of the Indian Wars* (1913). Facsimile presses have continued this reproduction in our own day. The best known tracts are as follows:

Easton, John. "A Relacion of the Indyan Warre," in Charles H. Lincoln (ed.), *Narratives of the Indian Wars, 1675-1699*, (New York, 1913), pp. 1-17. Reprinted New York, 1946.

A Farther Brief and True Narration of the Late Wars Risen in New England. London, 1676. This newsletter, dated December 28, 1675, has been reproduced in facsimile by the Society of Colonial Wars in New England. It was included in Samuel G. Drake, *The Old Indian Chronicle,* Boston 1867.

Gookin, Daniel. "An Historical Account of the Doings and Sufferings of the Christian Indians in New England, in the years of 1675, 1676, 1677," in *Transactions and Collections of the American Antiquarian Society,* II (Cambridge, 1836), pp. 423-534.

Harris, William. "Letter to Sir Joseph Williamson, August 12, 1676," *Collections of the Rhode Island Historical Society,* Vol. X (Providence, 1902), pp. 162-79.

[Harris, William] Leach, D. E. (ed.), *A Rhode Islander Reports on King Philip's War, the Second William Harris Letter of August 1676*. Providence, R.I. Hist. Soc., 1963.

Hubbard, William. *A Narrative of the Troubles with the Indians in New-England*. Boston, 1677. Republished under the title, *The Present State of New-England,* London, 1677. Republished by Samuel G. Drake under the title, *The History of the Indian Wars in New England from the First Settlement to the Termination of the War with King Philip, in 1677.* 2 Vols., Roxbury, Mass., 1865. Reprinted by Burt Franklin, "Woodward's Historical Series," vol. III. New York, 1971.

[Hutchinson, Richard] *The Warr in New-England Visibly Ended.* London, 1677. Republished in Samuel G. Drake, *The Old Indian Chronicle, op. cit.*; in Charles H. Lincoln, *op. cit.;* also in *King Philip's War Narratives.* "March of America Facsimile Series," No. 29. Ann Arbor, Michigan, 1966.

Mather, Increase. *A Brief History of the Warr with the Indians in New England.* Boston and London, 1676. Republished by Samuel G. Drake under the title, *The History of King Philip's War.* Boston, 1862.

—— *A Relation of the Troubles Which Have Hapned* [*sic*] in New-England. By Reason of the Indians There. *From the Year 1614 to the Year 1675.* Boston, 1677. Edited by Samuel G. Drake under the title *Early History of New England.* Albany, 1864.

"News from New-England, being a True and Last Account of the Present Bloody Wars." London, 1676. Reprinted in Samuel G. Drake, *Old Indian Chronicle, op. cit.*

Rowlandson, Mary. "Narrative of the Captivity of Mrs. Mary Rowlandson," in Charles H. Lincoln, *op. cit.* pp. 107-67.

[Saltonstall, Nathaniel] "The Present State of New England with Respect to the Indian War. 20 June to 10 November, 1675."

—— "A Continuation of the State of New England. 10 November, 1675 to 8 February, 1676."

—— "A New and Further Narrative of the State of New England. March to August 1676."

These three tracts were republished in Samuel G. Drake, *The Old Indian Chronicle, op. cit.*; in Charles H. Lincoln *op. cit.;* and in *King Philip's War Narratives, op. cit.*

A True Account of the Most Considerable Occurrences That Have Happened in the Warre between the English and the Indians in New England London, 1676. Reprinted in Samuel G. Drake, *The Old Indian Chronicle, op. cit.* and in *King Philip's War Narratives, op. cit.*

Wheeler, Thomas. *A True Narrative of the Lord's Providences in Various Dispensations towards Captain Edward Hutchinson of Boston and Myself, and Those that Went with Us into the Nipmuck Country*. Boston, 1675. Republished in *Collections of the New-Hampshire Historical Society*, Vol. II, Concord, 1827, pp. 5-23, and in *Old South Leaflets*, Vol. VII., No. 155.

[Williams, Roger] *A Copy of a Letter of Roger Williams, Telling of the Burning of Providence and of His Conference with the Indians during King Philip's War in 1676*. Edited by Bradford F. Swan for the Society of Colonial Wars and the Rhode Island Historical Society. Providence, 1971.

2. REFERENCE WORKS

Baylies, Francis. *An Historical Memoir of the Colony of New Plymouth.* Samuel G. Drake, ed. 2 vols. Boston, 1866. Successor to the 1830 edition. Part III is a narrative history of King Philip's War based on the contemporary accounts.

Bodge, George Madison. *Soldiers in King Philip's War.* Boston, 1906.

Boston Prints and Print Makers, 1670-1775; A Conference Held by the Colonial Society of Massachusetts, 1 and 2 April 1971. Published in Boston by the Colonial Society of Massachusetts and distributed by the University Press of Virginia, Charlottesville, Virginia, 1973.

Bowen, Richard LeBaron. *Early Rehoboth,* Vol. III. Rehoboth, 1948.

Brigham, Clarence S. *Paul Revere's Engraving.* Worcester, Mass.: American Antiquarian Society; New York: Atheneum Press, 1969.

Douglas-Lithgow, Robert A. *Dictionary of American-Indian Place and Proper Names in New England.* Salem, 1909.

Drake, Samuel G. *The Book of the Indians of North America.* Boston, 1851. Eleventh edition.

Fessenden, Guy Mannering. *History of Warren, Rhode Island, from the Earliest Times; with particular Notices of Massasoit and his Family.* Providence, 1845.

Little Compton Families. Published by the Little Compton Historical Society from Records Compiled by Benjamin Franklin Wilbour. Little Compton, R. I., 1967.

Monro, W. H., *History of Bristol R. I.: The Story of the Mount Hope Lands.* Providence, 1880.

Notes on Little Compton. Published by the Little Compton Historical Society from Records Compiled by Benjamin Franklin Wilbour. Edited by Carlton C. Brownell. Little Compton, R. I., 1970.

3. MODERN INTERPRETATIONS

(a) Books.

Abbott, John S. C. *History of King Philip.* New York, 1875.

Britt, Albert. *Great Indian Chiefs.* New York, 1938.

Burke, Charles T. *Puritans at Bay: The War Against King Philip and the Squaw Sachems.* New York, 1967.

Chapin, Howard M. *Sachems of the Narragansetts.* Providence: Rhode Island Historical Society, 1931.

Ellis, George W., and John E. Morris. *King Philip's War.* New York, 1906.

Jennings, Francis. "The Invasion of America: Myths and Strategies of English Colonialism in the Conquest of the Indians." To be published by the Institute of Early American History and Culture, Williamsburg, Virginia, in 1975.

Josephy, Alvin M., Jr. *The Patriot Chiefs: A Chronicle of American Indian Resistance.* New York, 1961.

Langdon, George D., Jr., *Pilgrim Colony, A History of New Plymouth 1620-1691.* New Haven, 1966.

Leach, D. E. *Flintlock and Tomahawk, New England in King Philip's War.* New York, 1958.

Lurie, Nancy and Leacock, Eleanor. *North American Indians in Historical Perspective.* New York, 1971.

Peirce, Ebenezer W. *Indian History, Biography and Genealogy pertaining to the Good Sachem Massasoit of the Wampanoag Tribe and his Descendants.* North Abington, Mass. Published by Zerviah Gould Mitchell, 1878.

Sheehan, Bernard W. *Seeds of Extinction: Jeffersonian Philanthropy and the American Indian.* Chapel Hill, 1974.

Simmons, W. S. Cauntantowwit's House: An Indian Burial Ground on the Island of Conanicut in Narragansett Bay . . . Providence, 1970.

Smith, J. M. S. *Seventeenth Century America, Essays in Colonial History.* Chapel Hill, 1959.

Strock, Daniel, Jr. *Pictorial History of King Philip's War.* Boston. 1852.

Travers, Milton A. *The Wampanoag Federation of the Algonquin Nation.* New Bedford, 1957.

Vaughan, Alden T. *New England Frontier: Puritans and Indians 1620-1675*. Boston, 1965.

Woodward, Carl R. *Plantation in Yankeeland.* Pequot Press (Chester, Conn.). 1971.

(b) Pamphlets and Articles

Frost, J. W. "Saints and Savages: The Puritan's Conception of the Indian," Unpublished M.A. Thesis, University of Wisconsin.

Gahan, Laurence K. "The Nipmucks and their Territory," *Bulletin of the Massachusetts Archaeological Society,* July 1941.

Jennings, Francis. "Goals and Functions of Puritan Missions to the Indians," *Ethnohistory,* Vol. XVIII, No. 3, (1971), pp. 197-212.

—— "Virgin Land and Savage People," *American Quarterly,* Vol. XXIII, No. 4, (1971), pp. 519-541.

Knowles, Nathaniel. "The Torture of Captives by the Indians of Eastern North America," *Proceedings of the American Philosophical Society,* Vol. LXXXII, (1940), pp. 151-225.

Malone, Patrick M. "Indian Military Technology," *American Quarterly,* Vol. XXV (1), pp. 48-63.

Marten, Catherine. *The Wampanoags in the Seventeenth Century: An Ethnohistorical Survey,* "Occasional papers in Old Colony Studies," No. 2, December 1970.

Robbins, Maurice. *The Indian History of Attleboro.* Attleboro Historical Commission. 1969.

Salisbury, Neal. "Red Puritans: The 'Praying Indians' of Massachusetts Bay and John Eliot," *William and Mary Quarterly,* January 1974.

Speck, Frank G. "Native Tribes and Dialects of Connecticut: A Mohegan-Pequot Diary," *Bureau of American Ethnology*, 43rd Annual Report, 1914-1925, pp. 199-287.

——— *Territorial Subdivisions and Boundaries of the Wampanoag, Massachusett, and Nauset Indians.* "Indian Notes and Monographs," No. 44. New York, 1928.

Swan, Bradford F. *An Indian's an Indian; or, the Several Sources of Paul Revere's Engraved Portrait of King Philip.* Providence: Roger Williams Press, 1959.

Vaughan, Alden T. "Pequots and Puritans: the Causes of the War of 1637." *William and Mary Quarterly* Vol. XXI, (April 1964), pp. 256-269.

Warner, R. A. "Southern New England Indians to 1725." Unpublished Ph.D. thesis (1935). Yale University Library.

Washburn, Wilcomb E. "History, Anthropology and the American Indian," *American Studies: An International Newsletter* Vol. XI, No. 1, Autumn 1972.

——— "Indian Wars in New England and Virginia," to be published in the forthcoming *Handbook of North American Indians.*

4. BIBLIOGRAPHIES

For comprehensive guides to all sources see, D. E. Leach, *Flintlock and Tomahawk: New England in King Philip's War,* (New York, 1958), pp. 271-90, and A. T. Vaughan, *New England Frontier: Puritans and Indians,* (Boston 1965), pp. 401-20.

The William Pabodie House at Little Compton.

NOTES TO INTRODUCTION

1. Charles H. Lincoln (ed.), *Narratives of the Indian Wars, 1675-1699* (New York, 1913), pp. 150, 156-57.

2. John Josselyn, "An Account of Two Voyages to New England," *Mass. Hist. Soc. Coll.*, 3d ser., Vol. III (1833), p. 310.

3. Samuel G. Drake (ed.), *The History of the Indian Wars* . . . (2 vols. Roxbury, Mass., 1865) Vol. II, p. 276.

4. See below, p. 16.

5. Samuel G. Drake (ed.), *The History of the Indian Wars, op. cit.*, Vol. I, p. 47.

6. No one knows with any real certainty what theories of land ownership were held by either the Indians or the Colonists, or how consistently they tried to follow them. The whole subject is deeply obscure and highly controversial. It has been argued that if the Indians did not originally understand the idea of an exclusive individual ownership in land it was soon forced on their understanding by the English. English ideas about the purchase, ownership and sale of lands in New England before King Philip's War have been interpreted with more or less sympathy according to the taste of the historian. For a recent indictment of English opportunism, chicanery and intimidation in land transactions with the Indians, see Francis Jennings, "Virgin Land and Savage People," *American Quarterly*, Vol. XXIII (October, 1971), pp. 519-41.

7. This illustration assumes the usual interpretation of the facts in this sensational case. It is possible, though unlikely,

that Philip and his men had nothing to do with the death of Sassamon.

8. Letter from John Robinson, at Leyden, Dec. 19, 1623 to Governor William Bradford. Quoted S.E. Morison (ed.), *Of Plymouth Plantation, 1620-1647* (New York, 1952), pp. 374-75.

9. i.e., "more than the Indians agreed to."

10. Charles H. Lincoln (ed.), "A Relacion of the Indyan Warre, by John Easton, 1675," in *Narratives, op. cit.*, pp. 10-12. Text has been modernized.

11. Samuel Eliot Morison put it in these terms, with his usual trenchancy, in his Introduction to D.E. Leach, *Flintlock and Tomahawk* (New York, 1958).

12. See H. M. Dexter, *The History of King Philips War, By Benjamin Church* (Boston, 1865), Part II, pp. xxv-xxxi; and Samuel G. Drake, *History of the Indian Wars, op. cit.*, Part I, p. 59, note 101; and p. 265, note 412.

13. See below, p. 29.

14. D.E. Leach (ed.), *A Rhode Islander Reports on King Philip's War* (Providence: R. I. Hist. Soc., 1963), p. 61.

15. Missionaries to the Indians who visited Little Compton in 1698 reported two communities of Indians, one at Sakonnet, the other at Acoaxet, each with their rulers and teachers. In 1700 there were said to be one hundred Indian men living in Little Compton, which would make the size of the tribe about four hundred—a higher figure than seems likely. Many died of a fever about 1750. In 1774, the census reported one man and thirteen women above the age of sixteen, five boys and six girls. By 1803 there were not more than ten left; the death of the last member of the tribe, Sarah Howdee, was reported in the *Providence Journal* of May 7, 1827. Dexter, *op. cit.*, Part I, p. 85.

16. Walker's Roadside Stand marks the scene where the first land in Little Compton was cleared by Benjamin Church. This was Lot 19. The schoolhouse on the east

side of the road, which Dexter cited in his 1865 edition to identify Church's lot, is now (1975) occupied by Mr. Clayton Lester. See below p. 38.

17. See below, p. 38.

18. Dexter, *op. cit.*, Part I, p. 85.

19. *Ibid.*, Part I, pp. xxxviii-xli.

20. Cotton Mather, *Magnalia Christi Americana*, 2d ed. (Hartford, 1820), Vol. II, p. 499.

21. Dexter, *op. cit.*, Part I, pp. xxxviii-xli.

22. See below, p. 44.

23. The "Minutes," Commissions and other records which were in Benjamin Church's possession when his memoirs were prepared for the press are presumably lost. One or two of his personal possessions, such as his sword, have survived, but no traces of his papers have been found. It is possible that a thorough search of the public records would tell us more about the field reports that he made during the war.

24. Dexter, *op. cit.*, Part II, p. 148.

25. See below, p. 52.

26. Among the American libraries known to possess the very rare first edition are the following: John Carter Brown Library, Brown University, Providence, R.I.; the Boston Public Library; the Widener Library, Harvard; the Essex Institute, Salem, Mass.; the Library of Congress; the Newberry Library, Chicago; the William L. Clements Library, University of Michigan, and the Henry E. Huntington Library, San Marino, Cal.

27. Dexter, *op. cit.*, Part I, p. ix.

28. E.S. Morgan, *The Gentle Puritan. A Life of Ezra Stiles, 1725-1795* (New Haven, Yale University Press, 1962), pp. 136-39; F. B. Dexter, *Itineraries and Correspondence of Ezra Stiles* (New Haven, Yale University Press, 1916).

29. This grandson was Deacon Benjamin Church of Boston.

son of Edward Church. According to Dexter, he described himself in his letter to Stiles as "almost too old for such juvenile attempts [i.e., as the Latin ode in glorification of his grandfather], being upwards of 67." (Dexter, *op. cit.*, Part I, p. x.) Another quotation from this letter, which is said to have been written in April 1772, explains that grandson Benjamin had lived with his grandfather Benjamin from his infancy up to the 'old man's death—about eleven years. (*New England Historical and Genealogical Register,* Vol. XI, p. 155.) Roswell B. Burchard, descendent of Joseph Church, seems to refer to the same letter in his "Historical Address" of 1904: "Among my most valued possessions is a long letter written to the Rev. Ezra Stiles of Newport by the grandson of Col. Benjamin Church, in which he gives a personal description of his grandfather and an account of his fatal fall from his horse," *Bi-centennial Celebration of the United Congregational Church of Little Compton.* (1904), p. 62. We have been unable to locate this letter. Presumably Stiles incorporated all the essential information about Colonel Church in the short "life" which he printed in his edition.

30. Charles Deane, *Proc. of the Mass. Hist. Soc.*, ser. I, vol. XIX, pp. 243-45; H. M. Dexter, *op. cit.*, Part I, p. xliii.

31. Bradford F. Swan, *An Indian's an Indian; or the Several Sources of Paul Revere's Engraved Portrait of King Philip* (Providence, 1959).

32. See below, p. 53.

33. Samuel G. Drake, "Portraits and Bibliographical Reminiscences," *Historical Magazine,* Vol. IV 2d ser., no. 6 (1868).

34. For a list of Drake's editions and re-issues, see below, p. 59.

35. The simile is Church's own. See p. 61.

36. See p. 62.

37. Dexter, *op. cit.*, Part I, p. 174, note 360.

38. See "Suggestions for Reading."

39. Dexter, *op. cit.*, Part II, p. 15, note 24.

40. *Ibid*, p. 125, note 266.

41. W. J. Miller. *Notes concerning the Wampanoag Tribe of Indians* (Providence, 1880), p. 94.

42. It is possible that a precise textual comparison of Church's narrative with all the narratives whose publication preceded his might indicate that he had access to other sources besides his own records and recollections. If so, this evidence eluded H.M. Dexter, his most meticulous editor.

43. Dexter gives us an opportunity to compare in detail a field report of Church's with his later description in his memoirs of the same events, but the reference is to the Eastern Expedition of 1690. Dexter, *op. cit.*, Part II, pp. 50-65.

44. See p. 72.

NOTES TO TEXT

Most of the following notes are a shortened version of H. M. Dexter's voluminous ones.

1. Now mainly Tiverton, Rhode Island, including the eastern shore of Mount Hope Bay from Fall River on the north to Pachet Brook on the south.

2. Now spelled Sakonnet. Mainly Little Compton, Rhode Island, extending from Pachet Brook to the ocean.

WITH AWASHONKS, QUEEN OF THE SAKONNETS

1. Indian name for Plymouth.

2. Little Eyes and his family threw in their lot with Philip. When he was captured later in the war, Church was urged to revenge himself for this incident, but replied, "it was not Englishmen's fashion to seek revenge" (see p 133 , below)

WITH WEETAMOO, QUEEN OF THE POCASSETS

1. Tiverton heights, which the old road to Fall River climbs after leaving the Stone Bridge.

2. H. M. Dexter estimated that going by Indian paths, Plymouth might have been forty-two miles from Pocasset and nearly fifty from Church's house at Sakonnet.

3. The narrow strip, between the Kickemuit and Warren rivers, which joins the peninsula of Mount Hope (Pockanocket) to the mainland at Swansea.

4. 20 June 1675.

THE MOUNT HOPE CAMPAIGN

1. William Bradford, second son of the famous Governor William Bradford.

2. James Cudworth. Over seventy at this time, he was made Commander-in-Chief.

3. 22 June 1675.

4. The fortified house of the Rev. John Myles, pastor of the Baptist church in Swansea. It was his meeting house to which the settlers in Mount Hope Neck had gone on 22 June 1675, when Philip's Indians plundered their houses in the first action of the war.

5. The Massachusetts forces, which had arrived by 28 June, included a troop of horse under Captain Thomas Prentice, a troop of foot under Captain Daniel Henchman, one hundred and ten "volunteers" under Captain Samuel Mosley (among them a dozen pirates released from their death cells), three Christian Indians as guides, and some hunting dogs.

6. The small peninsula running into Mount Hope Bay, now called Gardner's Neck.

7. 29 June 1675.

8. 30 June 1675.

9. Constant Southworth, Church's father-in-law.

PEASE FIELD FIGHT

1. Also called Pocasset Neck. Projects southward and westward from the mainland of Tiverton. Entered today from Tiverton Four Corners.

2. i.e., Church's brother-in-law, William (Bill) Southworth.

3. The reference to these black rocks was carelessly dropped in the second edition (1772) and rediscovered by Dexter in the first edition (1716). It helped him to identify the site of the fight at the junction of Fogland Point with Punkatees Neck. Church's Well survives.

4. A resident of Portsmouth, Rhode Island, Captain Golding was the owner of a vessel which was much used to transport troops during the war. Plymouth Colony rewarded him with one

hundred acres of land. Highly regarded by Church, he was with him at the killing of Philip.

5. 9 July 1675.

6. Alderman, a subject of Weetamoo, was the Indian who was to kill Philip.

HUNTING WEETAMOO AND PHILIP

1. They were on their way to the Bristol ferry, which could take them over to Rhode Island, and then over Howland's ferry to Pocasset. From there (now the Stone Bridge) they would have gone north to the Cedar Swamp, about two miles south of Fall River, where Weetamoo was camped.

2. Captain Hunter, a Christianized Nipmuck Indian, was one of 52 "praying Indians" who had just been sent to the army at Mount Hope on orders from Massachusetts.

3. Hubbard describes how, at the end of July, Philip was run down to a Pocasset swamp but then escaped across the Taunton River (near Fall River) into the Nipmuck country.

THE GREAT SWAMP FIGHT

1. Over a thousand men were raised—six companies from Massachusetts, five from Connecticut, two from Plymouth, and some recruits from Rhode Island.

2. An officer whose command has been abolished ("reformed") but who continues to do regimental duties.

3. Major Smith's block-house was on the Pequot road to the north of Wickford Hill, in North Kingston, Rhode Island. Church took the nearest route across the ferries (either Bristol to Rhode Island to Conanicut to Wickford; or Bristol to Prudence to Wickford) while the army went round by Providence and tried to surprise Pumham in his village at Warwick.

4. 11 December 1675.

5. 19 December 1675.

6. The fort was a stockade, enclosing five or six acres of upland in the middle of a swamp. The palisade was reinforced by a dense hedge. There were only two narrow entrances, each across a log.

7. The Connecticut forces included 150 Mohegans and Pequots, who, according to Captain James Oliver, "proved very false, fired into the air, and sent word before they came they would do so, but got much plunder, guns and kettles." S.G. Drake, *Book of the Indians*, p. 219.

CHURCH WOUNDED

1. On the English side it was estimated that about 68 were killed or died of their wounds (including Captains Johnson, Davenport, Gardner, Seeley, Gallup, Marshall and Mason) and that 150 recovered from wounds. The same source estimated that 300 Indian warriors were killed, and 350 captured, together with (or including?) 300 women and children. Other estimates of Indian casualties were higher.

IN THE NIPMUCK COUNTRY

1. Supposed by Dexter to be Pumham's town, in Warwick, Rhode Island.

2. "Netop" means "friend." Being often used by Englishmen as a way of greeting Indians, it came to mean "Indian."

3. The army returned to Boston February 5, 1676, after chasing Indians into the woods between Marlborough and Brookfield.

PHILIP'S MOVEMENTS AND CHURCH'S COUNSEL

1. Schaghticoke is on the Hudson and Hoosic rivers, 12 miles from Troy. There is other evidence of New England Indians having fled there. Increase Mather reported that Philip tried to embroil the Mohawks with the English by killing some Mohawks and blaming the English, only to have his plot exposed and recoil on himself.

2. 19 May 1676. Turner, sent to relieve the western towns, surprised the Indians at these falls while they were fishing, killing from 130 to 180. On returning from the expedition he was himself killed with 38 of his men.

3. Wachusett mountain, Princeton, Mass.

4. Church seems to have confused the order of events at this point. It was not the attack on Sudbury, of 21 April 1676, which produced this council of war, but the attacks on Lancaster and Medfield in February. Dexter (p. 66) suggests that this was the

Council of War which was held at Plymouth on February 29, 1676.

INTERLUDE IN RHODE ISLAND

1. Clark's Garrison was about three miles southeast of Plymouth on the west bank of the Eel River. It was destroyed by Totoson and ten Indians on Sunday, 12 March 1676, Mrs. Clark and ten others being killed.

2. Captain Pierce, who was in command of 63 Englishmen and 20 friendly Indians, met Church on March 9. On March 26 he was killed with 51 of his English and 11 of his Indians at Rehoboth.

3. Church left Plymouth on March 8 or 9 and reached Captain Almy's house, which was on the Portsmouth shore opposite Fogland, on March 11, 1676.

4. Constant Church

5. Falmouth, Massachusetts

6. 6 June 1676.

ADOPTION OF THE CHURCH STRATEGY

1. Providence was burned March 30, 1676. Roger Williams describes his conference with the marauding Indians on this occasion in Bradford F. Swan (ed.), *A Copy of a Letter of Roger Williams* (Providence, 1971).

2. From Falmouth, past the Elizabeth Islands, to Sakonnet Point would be a canoe trip of about 35 miles.

MEETING ON SAKONNET POINT

1. Tompe Swamp, on the north side of the present Swamp Road, encompassing Wilbour Woods.

2. Nompash was to serve as Captain of the Sakonnet Indians in Church's Eastern Expedition of 1689.

3. Captain Edward Richmond was an original proprietor of Little Compton. The rock is famous as "Treaty Rock."

4. i.e., to Captain Almy's house, near the Portsmouth landing of Fogland Ferry.

5. i.e., who paddled him from Falmouth.

PARLEY AT TREATY ROCK

1. "Wetuset" is Mount Wachusett, where Philip had quartered. "Occapechees" can be translated "drams" or "tots": the literal meaning is "little strong drinks."

2. 25 June 1676. Peter, George and about 30 Sakonnet Indians appeared before the Plymouth Council on 28 June and made a submission which was accepted.

3. 27 June 1676.

4. Sachuest Neck, point of land directly opposite and three miles west of Sakonnet Point.

5. Nonquit, the pond lying between Punkatees Neck and Tiverton.

SUBMISSION OF AWASHONKS AT PUNKATEES

1. 30 June 1676. According to both William Hubbard and Increase Mather about 90 Indians accompanied her.

2. 1 July 1676.

3. The narrow entrance of the Kickemuit River, separating Bristol from Warren.

4. Probably July 6, 1676.

5. Now Wareham.

6. Runs into Buzzard's Bay between Wareham and Marion

7. According to Dexter, the eastern and southern shore of Mattapoisett. (Dexter I, 96).

A NEW COMMISSION

1. The Commission printed here may be the "enlarged" commission referred to on page 129 below.

RUNNING DOWN THE ENEMY

1. Middleborough—10 miles west of Plymouth, whose Indian name was Namasket.

2. Probable date of expedition: 20-27 July 1676.

3. Tuspaquin, alias the Black Sachem, was Sachem of Assawompset, Middleborough. He had been involved in land sales

with John Sassamon and with Benjamin Church before the war. His son was convicted of Sassamon's murder. Took part in the burning of Scituate, 20 April 1676, and Bridgewater, 8 May 1676.

4. The settlement at the head of the Acushnet inlet, three miles north of New Bedford. Incorporated with Ponagansett and Coke-sit into the Township of Dartmouth in 1664, it had been burnt in the summer of 1675.

CAPTURE OF LITTLE EYES

1. Probably Palmer's Island

2. Lightfoot had volunteered at Mattapoiset (p 133). Church later made him a captain and took him on his first Eastern Expedition, in 1689.

RAIDING IN THE GREAT CEDAR SWAMP

1. Near the present North Dartmouth.

2. Son of Francis Cook; arrived on the Mayflower; married Sarah Warren, sister of Church's mother, Elizabeth Warren; a first settler of Acushnet and deputy for many years.

3. William Forbes, son of a Duxbury settler who was one of the founders of Bridgewater, married Elizabeth Southworth, younger sister of Church's wife, Alice. Settled in Little Compton and served on Church's Third Expedition in 1692.

4. Dexter says this was probably Jonathan Delano, son of Philip who arrived in the *Fortune* in 1621 and was one of the first settlers of Duxbury.

5. Peleg Sanford, a leading citizen and soldier who lived in what is now Middletown, then Newport, about eight miles down the Island from Tripp's ferry. Was with Church at the killing of Philip. Succeeded Cranston as Governor in 1680.

PHILIP AND QUINNAPIN

1. One of his wives was a sister of Philip's wife, Wootone-kanuske. Another was Weetamoo, Queen of the Pocassets. Fought in the Great Swamp Fight where he seems to have been second-in-command to Canonchet. Also in the attack on Lancaster, 10 February 1675, where Mrs. Rowlandson was captured; he bought her from her captor and features in her narrative with

Weetamoo as her master and mistress. Court-martialled and shot at Newport, 25 August 1676.

2. Possibly Pumham, who was killed at Dedham 25-27 July, 1676.

3. Two or three miles north-west of New Bedford.

4. Southern part of Fairhaven on eastern boundary of New Bedford Harbor.

TACTICS OF INDIAN WARFARE

1. Major Bradford was commanding Plymouth's troops; Captains Brattle, Moseley and Henchman had companies of Massachusetts' troops; Major Talcott commanded 250 English and 200 Mohegans from Connecticut.

2. 30 July 1676.

3. Dexter explains why he thinks this was Monday evening, 31 July and not Sunday evening. (I, 124-25).

4. Unkompoin—Dexter's spelling.

5. 1 August 1676.

CAPTURE OF PHILIP'S WIFE AND SON

1. The Court consulted the Elders about the disposal of Philip's son, and were advised, on scriptural models, that he might be justly killed. His life was spared, and he and his mother, Wootonekanuske were sold into slavery either at Cadiz or in the West Indies.

2. Takanumma, according to Dexter, (I, 129).

3. 2 August 1676.

PHILIP'S FORCES ROUTED NEAR BRIDGEWATER

1. Isaac Howland, youngest son of John, was brother of Jabez and one of the first settlers of Middleborough.

2. Hubbard and Mather tell the same story, in their contemporary narratives, but say that it was one of Church's Indians who shouted the warning. Church did not speak Indian.

3. According to Dexter, who summarized his convictions in a footnote which occupied all but three lines of the page, this was the fitting end of a memorably drunken life. (I, 135).

4. According to Hubbard, Church's own force consisted of no more than "30 Englishmen and 20 reconciled Christians."

5. 4 August 1676.

6. 7 August 1676.

7. Sam Barrow is said to have been Totoson's father.

DEATH OF TOTOSON

1. Totoson's fame—or infamy, as the Colonists would say—came chiefly from his daring raid on Clark's Garrison on Sunday morning, 12 March 1676, while most of the residents were at church. This supposedly impregnable garrison on the outskirts of Plymouth was totally destroyed and its occupants, including Mrs. Clark, murdered.

2. 11 August 1676.

3. Sandy Point was on the Bristol side of the Bristol ferry. Abiol Tripp, who lived on the Portsmouth side, was running this ferry at the end of the seventeenth century.

PHILIP KILLED

1. i.e., pouch, in which the Indian carried his meal.

2. Probably Caleb Cook, grandson of Mayflower Francis Cook. According to family tradition, he traded his gun for the Indian's gun that shot Philip. From his descendants in Kingston, Mass., the lock made its way to the Massachusetts Historical Society and the barrel to the Pilgrim Society in Plymouth.

3. Alderman. See above.

4. Meaning, "Fight! Fight!"

5. Probably Peter, son of Awashonks.

6. In ordering the beheading and quartering of Philip, Church was executing in the field the sentence which English law required for treason. Philip's head was carried to Plymouth where it was placed on a pole and remained exposed for a generation. Cotton Mather tells how on a certain occasion he "took off the jaw from the exposed skull of that blasphemous leviathan." Philip's quarters were hung on four trees. Dexter reminds us that at the Restoration of King Charles II in 1660, Parliament voted that the bodies of Oliver Cromwell and two other regicides should be disinterred, hanged at Tyburn, and their heads placed

on poles at Westminster Hall. It was not until the nineteenth century that such practices became offensive to the idea of human dignity.

7. 12 August 1676.

THE SEARCH FOR ANNAWON

1. 6 or 7 September 1676.

2. Projects from the western side of Bristol into the bay.

3. i.e., what signal of the tribe to use.

4. 11 September 1676.

5. The fort on the Kickemuit whose construction Church had criticized the previous summer.

THE CAPTURE OF ANNAWON

1. On the eastern side of Rehoboth.

2. Asuhmequn—Massasoit's other name.

3. Caleb Cook, who had missed being the killer of Philip.

4. The approach to Annawon's Rock can be found today on Route 44, between Taunton and Rehoboth, about six miles west of Taunton.

5. i.e., "Who's there?"

6. i.e., "It is well." Literally, "It is satisfactory."

PHILIP'S REGALIA

1. Mohawk's country.

2. Philip's regalia were presented by Josiah Winslow, Governor of Plymouth, to King Charles II in a letter of 26 June 1677, which asked the king to accept, " . . . these few Indian rarities, beeing the best of our spoyles, and the best of the ornaments and treasure of sachem Philip the grand Rebell, the most of them taken from him by Capt. Benjamin Church (a person of great loyalty and the most successful of our commanders) when hee was slayne by him; being his Crowne, his gorge, and two belts of theire owne makeing of their golde and silver." (Dexter, *op. cit.*, I, 174). A later letter of the Governor to a royal secretary in 1680 indicates that these regalia had not yet reached the King because

they were being detained in Ferries Hall, Essex, by the Governor's brother-in-law. Major Waldegrave Pelham. (Charles T. Burke, *Puritans at Bay* [New York, 1967], p. 228.)

TUSPAQUIN, LAST OF PHILIP'S CAPTAINS

1. Powwow, variously interpreted as priest, medicine man, sorcerer, or witch-doctor. Hubbard comments sardonically that "he fell down at the first shot" when the Plymouth authorities tested his impenetrability. For Tuspaquin's previous history see footnote 3 above.

2. Church's error—he did not die until 16 March 1679.

3. The Court met 1 November 1676.

4. January 1677, by our calendar.

NOTES: MYTHICAL HISTORY OF KING PHILIP (APPENDIX I)

1. Samuel G. Drake, "Portraits and Biographical Reminiscences," *Historical Magazine,* Vol. IV, 2d ser., no. 6 (1868).

2. See illustration, p. 164.

3. Illustrated in *R. I. Hist. Soc. Coll.,* Vol. XXIV, no. 1 (Jan. 1931), p. 63. See also *R. I. Hist. Soc. Coll., 1874-75,* "Report of Northern Department," pp. 60-61.

4. See illustration, p. 165. Presented to the Massachusetts Historical Society by Isaac Lothrop in 1803 and transferred to the Peabody Museum in 1927. See Charles C. Willoughby, *Antiquities of the New England Indians* (Cambridge, Mass., 1935), pp. 427-28.

5. Edmund Burke Delabarre, *Dighton Rock: A Study of the Written Rocks of New England* (New York, 1928), pp. 257-58. Fig. 88.

6. Frederick J. Dockstader, *The American Indian Observed* (New York, 1971), illustration no. 62.

7 For Lydia Tuspaquin, see illustration, p. 178. For Emma Stafford, her daughter, see negative no. 12220 in the Museum of the American Indian: Heye Foundation, N.Y.C., and Frank Speck, *Territorial Subdivisions and Boundaries of the Wampanoag, Massachusett, and Nauset Indians,* "Indian Notes and Monographs," no. 44 (New York, 1928).

INDEX

This index is confined mainly to place names and proper names which are of interest to genealogists. These readers are urged to inspect the copious notes supplied by Dexter in the 1865 edition of this work.

A.

Acushnet, 132, 134; *see* Dartmouth
Agawam in Wareham, 124, 148-49, 172
Akkompoin, 141
Albany, 29, 92, 105
Alden, John, house in Duxbury, 37
Alderman, the slayer of Philip, 16, 90, 156
Alexander (Wamsutta), 6, 7, 22, his mark, 23; 26
Algonquians, 4
Almy, Captain John, 37, 67, 83, 107
Andover, 33
Annawon, 6, 16, 35, 36, 44, 59, 63, 154, 157-73
Apponegansett, 92
Assawampsett, Pond and Neck, 23, 73, 131, 138
Asuhmequn, *see* Massasoit
Awashonks, 7, 23, signature, 25; 34, 38, 69-73, 80, 111-15, 119, 120, 124, 125-27

B.

Barnes, John, 135
Barrow, Sam, 148
Baxter, Thomas, 91
Belcher, Captain Andrew, 77, 101
Bloody Brook, 31
Bradford, Major William, 34, 61, 75, 119, 120, 130-31
Bradford, Governor William, 37
Bridgewater, 33, 131, 140-41, 143-45, 147
Bristol, R. I., 38, 39, Benj. Church's house, 40; 118, 158

Brookfield, 29
Brown, James, 73-75
Brownell, Carlton, 43
Bump, John, 172
Burchard, John Church, 43

C.

Canonchet, 10, 33
Canonicus, 10
Cedar Swamp, *see* Great Cedar Swamp
Charles II, 59
Chelmsford, 33
Church, Alice Southworth, wife of Benjamin, 42, 107-08, 113
Church, Col. Benjamin, 36-43, *passim*; descendants of, 42-43
Church, Joseph, autograph, 180
Church, Richard, father of Benjamin, 36
Church's Well, 89
Church, Thomas, 39, 42, 43, 44, 107
Churchill, Charles, the poet, 52
Clark's Garrison, at Eel River, in Plymouth, 107, 130
Commission of Capt. Church, 128-29, 130, 175-76
Connecticut River, 31, 33, 34, 105
Conscience, of "Swanzey," 176
Cook, Caleb, 153, 211 n., 163
Cook, John, 134, 138
Cook's house, ruins, 134, 138
Council of War, 105-06
Cranston, John, Gov. of Rhode Island, 81
Cudworth, Capt. James, 75
Cushnet, *see* Acushnet

D.

Dartmouth, 31, 35, 92, 109, 148
Deane, Charles, 52
Deed signed by Awashonks, 25
Deerfield, 31
Deer Island, 35
Delano, Jonathan, 135-38
Descendants of Col. Church, 42-43

Dexter, Henry M., 29, 43, 52-57, portrait, 58; 61
Dodson, Jonathan, 135, 209n.
Drake, Samuel G., 29, 47, 53-54; editions listed, 182-84
Duxbury (Duxborough), 2, 37, 38, 39, 67, 107

E.

Earl, Ralph, 92
Easton's Narrative, 26-27
Edmunds, Andrew, 92
Eels, Samuel, 92
Eldridge, James, Samuel, and Thomas, 94
Eliot, John, 2, 13, 14, 35
Elizabeth Islands, 109
Endicott, John, 21
Enlistment, Indian manner of, 126-27

F.

Fall River, 38
"Falls Fight," 105
Falmouth, Mass., 108, 109
Fobes, William, 134, 209n.
Fogland Point, 84
Fuller, Matthew, 80-81, 82

G.

Gardner's Neck, in Mount-Hope Bay, see Mattapoisett
Gardner, Capt. Joseph, 95
George, 69, 111-14
Gill, John, 77
Golding, Capt. Roger, 88, 149-51, 153
Gookin, Daniel, 14
Gorton, Samuel, 73
Gould Island, 88
Gravestone of Col. Church, 177
Great Cedar Swamp (N. Dartmouth), 134-36
Great Swamp Fight, 32, 94-102; map, 96
Green, Bartholomew, 46
Groton, 10, 33
Gun that killed Philip, lock of, 154

H.

Hadley, 34
Hatfield, 31
Hathorne, Col., 61
Havens, Jack, 120-21, 125-26
Hazelton (Hastleton), Charles, 69
Hingham, 36
Honest George, see George
Howland, Isaac, 145
Howland, Jabez, 4, 124, 126, 147, 157
Hubbard, William, 6-7, 16, 29, 34, 59, 62
Hunter, Capt. John, 91
Hutchinson, Richard, 61

I.

Indian dance, 69-70, 126-27
Inventory of Col. Church's estate, 41-42
Irish, John, 38
Irish, Mrs. John, 39

J.

Jeffery, 129-30

K.

Kickemuit River, 6, 79
Kingston, 32

L.

Lake, David, 83
Lancaster, 33
Leach, Douglas, 56
Leverett, John, Gov., 2, 3, 23, 173
Lightfoot, 133, 137, 143, 158, 160
Little Compton, vii, First Purchase, 25; 35, 37, 38, 39, 65, 67
Little Eyes, 72, 132-33, 137
Low, Anthony, 118
Lucas, Benoni, 146

M.

Marlborough, 33
Marshfield, 140
Mason, Capt. John, 21
Massachusetts tribe, 11
Massasoit (Asuhmequin), 5, 6, 18, 19, 22, his mark, 23; 163, 171
Mattapoisett River, 138
Mattapoisett Neck (Gardner's Neck), in Swansea, 75, 79, 160
Mather, Increase, 16, 59
Matoonas, 10, 34
Medfield, 33
Mendon, 10, 31, 34
Metacomet, *see* Philip
Miantonomo, 10, 21
Middleborough, 31, 129, 130
Miles, *see* Myles
Mitchell, Zerviah, *see* Tuspaquin, Lydia
Mohawks, 105, 170
Mohegans, 11, 21
Monponset Pond, in Halifax, 129
Monoco (One-Eyed John), 10
Montaup, *see* Mount Hope
Mount Hope, 6, 22, 26, 30, 70, 74, Map 76; 150-57, 162
Mount Wachusett, *see* Wachusett
Muttaump, of Quabaug, 10
Myles Garrison, 75, 77, 89, 91
Myles, Rev. John, 75

N.

Namasket (Nemascut), *see* Middleborough
Nanaquaket Neck, 82
Narragansett Indians, 5, 10, 19, 20, 21, 26, 30, 31-33, 94-102, 105, 121, 129, 142-43
Nathaniel, 158-61
Natick, 11, 14
Nausets, 5
Netops, meaning of the word, 104, 206n.
New England settlements, 2
Newport, R. I., 35, 46, 112, 118
Niantics, 10

Ninigret, 10, 11, 32
Nipmucks, 5, 8, 31, 102-05
Nipsachuck, 31, 34
Nomquid, 119, 208n.
Northfield, 31
Northampton, 33
Numpas (Nompash), 112

O.

Occape, occapeeches, 114-15
Oldham, John, 20, 21

P.

Pabodie, William, 38, 196
Pachet Brook, 25, 38
Palfrey, John Gorham, 55
Pawtucket (Petuxit) River, 31, 92
"Pease-field Fight," 83-90
Pequots, 11, 116
Pequot War, 20-21, 36
Perkins, Mrs. Paul F., 43
Pessacus, 10
Peter Awashonks, 112, 118, 153
Peter Nunnuit, 7, 73-74
Petuxit, 108
Philip, 6, 22, 26-36, mark on a deed, 42; imaginary portraits, 47, 50-52, 60; 69-74, 79, 90, 92, 105, 121, 136, 138, 141, 142-47, 150-56, 170-71, 179-80
Philip's son, 142
Pierce, Capt. Michael, 107
Plymouth, General Court, 22, 108, 117, 173-74
Plymouth, 39, 127, 138, 140, 147-48, 149, 156-57, 172-73
Pocasset (Tiverton) 7, 38, 39, 67, 73, 79-90, 92, 119, 149, 158
Poneganset, 92, 133
Poppasquash Neck, in Bristol, 158-59
Portsmouth, 119
Pouwau, Powow, 173, 213n.
Prentice, Capt. Thomas, 77, 99
Proprietors of Sakonnet, 37-38
Providence, 31, 33, 108
Prudence Island, 158

Pumham, 10, 34, 94
Pumham's Town, *see* Warwick
Punkatees Neck (Punkateast, Punkateeset, Pocasset Neck), 83-90, 115-16, 119, 120

Q.

Quabaug, *see* Brookfield
Quaiapen, 10, 34
Quequechan River, *see* Fall River
Quinnapin (Qunnapin), 7, 10, 35, 136, 142

R.

Rattlesnakes, 82
Reformado, 94, 205n.
Rehoboth, 31, 33, 80, 94, 157, 163
Rehoboth Plain (Seekonk Plain), 92, 121
Revere, Paul, engraving of Philip, 47, 51-53; his model, 50; engraving of Church, 52-54
Richmond, Capt. John, 112
Robinson, John, 20
Rowlandson, Mrs. Mary, 7, 16
Russell's Garrison, 92
Russell's Orchard, 133

S.

Sabin (Sabine), 121
Sachueeset (Sachuest) Neck, 119, 208n.
Sakonnet (Little Compton), 39, map, 71; 82, 109, 111, 118-19
Sakonnet Indians, 7, 23, 26, 34, 69, 101-02, 109-27
Sagamore John, 29, 34
Sagamore Sam, *see* Shoshanim
Saltonstall, Nathaniel, 61
Sam Barrow, 148
Sandwich, 117, 120, 124, 149
Sandy Point (probably McCarry's Point on Portsmouth Shore), 84
Sanford, Major Peleg, 135, 209n., 149, 150, 153
Sassamon, John, 14, 23, 69, 73
Savage, Lieut. Perez, 79
Schaghticoke (Scattacook), 105
Scituate, 33, 151

Sconticut Neck, 137
Seconit (Sekonit), see Sakonnet
Sellers, John, Map of New England, 64
Shawomet, *see* Warwick
Shoshanim (Sagamore Sam), 10
Sippican, 138, 172
Sippican River, 124
Smith, John, 12
Smith, Major Richard, 94, 101
Smith's Garrison, 94, 101
Sogkonate, *see* Sakonnet
Sogkonesset, *see* Falmouth, Mass.
Southwick, Solomon, 46, 54
Southworth, Alice, 36; *see* Church, Alice; Southworth, B (probably Edward, Nathaniel, or William) 85
Southworth, Constant, 36, 38, 80, 121
Southworth, Elizabeth, 36
Southworth, Nathaniel, second son of Constant, 124
Sowams (Warren), 6, 22
Springfield, 31, 33
Squannakonk Swamp, in Rehoboth, 6, 162
Stafford, Emma, 180
Standish, Miles, 20
Stiles, Rev. Ezra, 39, 43, 46-47, 49, 54
Stone, Captain, 20-21
Stonington, 33
Sudbury, 33, 105
"Swamp Fight," *see* Great Swamp Fight
Swan, Bradford F., 52
Swansea, 22, 26, 31, 73, 75, 109, 157, 176
Sword, belonging to Benjamin Church, 40

T.

Takannumma, 143
Talcot, Major John, 147
Taunton, 22, 31, 75, 107, 130-31, 140, 147, 163, 169, 171
Taunton River, 34, 92, 139, 141
Taylor's Lane, 38
Thompson, Nathaniel, 38
Tispaquin, *see* Tuspaquin
Tiverton, *see* Pocasset
Tobias, 23
Toby, 121
Tompe Swamp, 7, 38, 111, 207n.

Totoson (Tatoson), 6, 36, 145-47, 148-49
Treaty Rock, in Little Compton, 113-17
Tripp, Abiel, his ferry, 150, 211n.
Turner, Captain William, 105
Tuspaquin, 6, 23, 131, 145, 172-73
Tuspaquin, Lydia, 180
Tyasks, 6, 138

U.

Uncas, 11, 21, 33
Unkompoin, 34

V.

Verelst, John, 52
Virginia, 12

W.

Wachusett Mountain (Wetuset), 10, 33, 105, 114
Wadsworth, Capt. Samuel, 105, 106
Walley, Major John, 61
Wampanoags, 5-6, *passim*
Wampum, the Indian currency, 171
Wamsutta, *see* Alexander
Warren, Elizabeth, 36
Warren, *see* Sowams
Warwick, 102, 108
Watuspaquin, *see* Tuspaquin
Weetamoo (Weetamore, Weetamoe), 7, 10, 31, 34, 73-74, 90-92, 121
Weymouth, 33
Wepoiset, 121
Wheeler, Thomas, 61
Whitin, Mrs. Richard C., 43
Wickford, 32
Wilbour Woods, *see* Tompe Swamp
Wilcox (Wilcockes), Daniel, 112
Williams, John (of Scituate), 151
Williams, Roger, 2, 13
Windmill Hill, 38
Winslow, Gov. Josiah, 2, 22, 32, 59, 72-74, 94, 100, 102, 107, 121, 123-24, 128-29, 174-76
Winslow, Penelope, 122
Winthrop, Gov. John, 2, 23, 36

Woosamequin, see Massasoit
Wootonekanuske (Philip's wife) 34, 142
Wrentham, 33

Y.

Yale University, 46
York, 105

This book was set by photo composition
in 11 point Baskerville with 3 point leading
designed and manufactured by Brush-Mill Books, Inc.

Diary of King Philip's War
By Benjamin Church

Edited by
Alan and Mary Simpson

Benjamin Church liked Indians and was liked by them. He studied them, admired them, jollied them, dealt fairly with them. He saw in them splendid fighters. They saw in him a splendid captain. He knew all about the Indian's "savagery," but he is untouched by the hatred and hysteria which fills the conventional history.

This is eye-witness history of the first great Indian War in North America, by the most successful guerilla captain on the English side. Behind his homespun stories of the Pease Field Fight, the Swamp Fight, the parleys with Queen Awashonks and the pursuit of King Philip lies a collision of cultures which set a pattern for almost all future relations between white men and red men in English America. If he could have foreseen the disappearance of the Indian from every swamp and beach in New England, he would have felt saddened.

This is the story of a warfare of extermination which nobody had planned; a description of sorties, ambushes, providential escapes and breath-taking victories which is written with all the immediacy and simplicity of folk art. Church's *Diary of King Philip's War* is one of the earliest and most graphic of American primitives.

About the editors—

English-born Alan Simpson was educated at Oxford and Harvard and served in the Royal Artillery for five years during World War II. He joined the faculty of the University of Chicago in 1946 where he became Thomas E. Donnelley Professor of History and Dean of the College. He has been President of Vassar College since 1964.

Mary McEldowney Simpson is a graduate of Knox College and Oxford University and the former Associate Editor of the *Bulletin of the Atomic Scientists.*

The Simpsons have a home in Little Compton where Benjamin Church was clearing the first homestead when King Philip's War began.

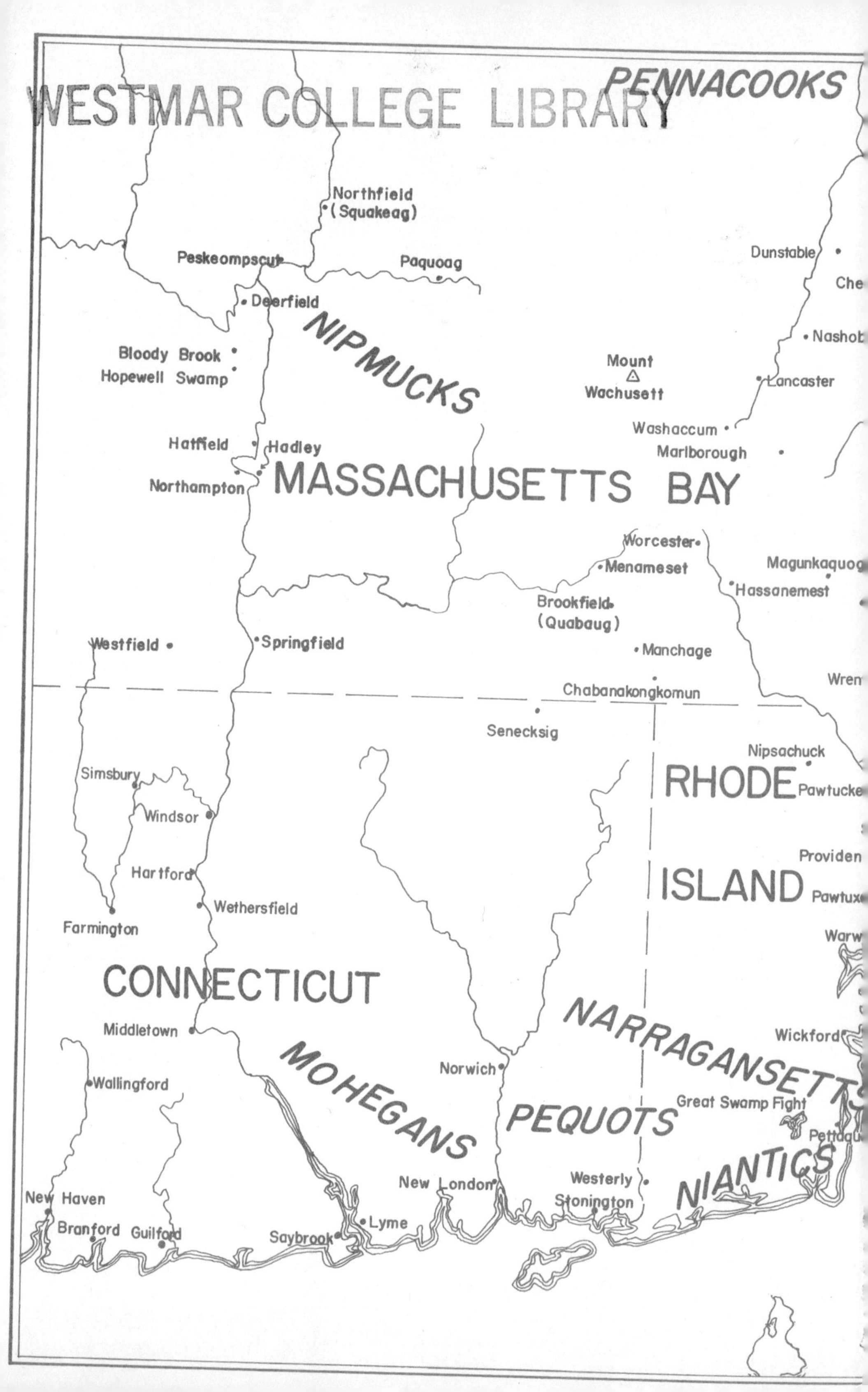
PENNACOOKS
Northfield
(Squakeag)
Peskeompscut
Paquoag
Dunstable
Deerfield
NIPMUCKS
Nashob
Bloody Brook
Hopewell Swamp
Mount
Wachusett
Lancaster
Washaccum
Marlborough
Hatfield
Hadley
Northampton
MASSACHUSETTS BAY
Worcester
Menameset
Magunkaquog
Hassanemest
Brookfield
(Quabaug)
Westfield
Springfield
Manchage
Chabanakongkomun
Wren
Senecksig
Nipsachuck
Simsbury
RHODE
Windsor
Providen
Hartford
ISLAND
Wethersfield
Farmington
CONNECTICUT
NARRAGANSETT
Middletown
Wickford
MOHEGANS
Norwich
Wallingford
Great Swamp Fight
PEQUOTS
New London
Westerly
NIANTICS
New Haven
Stonington
Branford
Guilford
Lyme
Saybrook